VENTURE MATHEMATICS WORKSHEETS

Blackline masters for higher ability classes aged 11-16

G. Geometry

Dr Christian Puritz

TarquinGroup
www.tarquingroup.com

© Tarquin and the Author 2005

ISBN 978 1 89961 871 2

Tarquin,   Distributed and printed in the USA by IPG Books
Suite 74, 17 Holywell Hill   www.ipgbook.com
St Albans,
AL1 1DT
United Kingdom

www.tarquingroup.com

A catalogue record for this book is available from the British Library.

Typesetting by Jane Adams
Cover illustration by George Noble

Printed in the UK and USA.

Preface

I wrote most of these worksheets while teaching at an English grammar (i.e. selective) school. Each sheet was motivated by a need felt at the time, to address inadequacies in text book exercises, to deal with new syllabus topics, or simply to follow out some idea. (Two or three have been written more recently for this collection.) They do not comprehensively cover any syllabus, but are provided as a resource to supplement textbooks and other available materials.

The sheets were written for class use in a selective school, so many of them include some fairly routine work, but most also have some hard questions to provide a challenge for the really able, who can get very frustrated when all the work they are given is easy. I have tried to provide guidance in the answer section to help with the hardest questions.

The sheets are classified into four sections: A for algebra and arithmetic, G for geometry, S for statistics, X for extra investigations. The biggest section is G: it just happened that way! (For the 16–18 age range I wrote a lot of statistics sheets, which I hope, God willing, to put together, with some notes on teaching the subject, in due course.)

Sheet G9 on Calculating π has appeared previously in *Mathematics in School*.

I am grateful to my publisher Andrew Griffin for giving much encouragement that spurred me on to do the considerable work involved in preparing the sheets for publication; and also to Jane Adams, the designer, who collaborated with great patience and efficiency in the layout of the final versions of the sheets.

Special thanks are due to my friend George Noble, who used his artistic gifts to produce far better diagrams than I could, as well as helping with the typing. He also, following an idea suggested by Mark Robins, produced the very politically incorrect cover design!

Last but not least, thanks to my wife Cynthia for her longsuffering during all this work, and for help with the checking. Any remaining errors are of course my responsibility. If you discover some and email me, cwpuritz@pmbx.net, I will be grateful, and will respond by sending you details of any other errors that have been found.

I hope you and your pupils will enjoy the venture!

Christian Puritz
January 2006

Contents

Other VMW's are available for:

- Algebra and Arithmetic
- Statistics and Xtra Investigations.

*This requires Cabri figures that can be downloaded from www.tarquinbooks.com – simply input VMW into the search box and download from the link on the product pages.

Areas, angles and constructions on graph paper

Use a new left hand page. Put the origin at the bottom left hand corner, and make *x* go from 0 to 16, *y* from 0 to 20; the scale unit is 1 cm. Use the right hand page for your answers. Draw and calculate the areas of the quadrilaterals and triangles given:

1   ABCD; A is (2, 19) B (2, 16)
        C (8, 16) D (8, 19)

2   ABC

3   CDE; E (15,16)

4   EFG; F (15, 18) G (12, 18)

5   HIJ; H (3, 15) I (2, 12) J (3, 12)

6   HJK; K(6,12)

7   HIK

8   LMN; L (10, 15) M (8, 12) N (15, 12)

9   PQR; P (2, 11) Q (2, 6) R (5, 8)

10 STU; S (12, 11) T (8, 6) U (12, 7)

11 VWXY; V (5, 5) W (2, 1) X(10, 1) Y (13, 5)

12 XYZ; Z (16, 0); to do this put a rectangular 'crate' round the triangle, with horizontal and vertical sides, as in the diagram, and subtract from the area of the crate the areas of the three triangles of 'packing' which surround triangle *XYZ*.

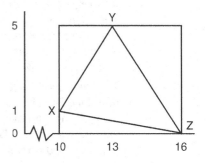

Now start a new left hand page, with axes and scales as before. Construct altitudes for each shape, use them to calculate estimates of the area, and also use the exact "crate – packing" method described in no.12. Measure all the angles in each figure and give the sum of the angles in each case.

13 ABC; A (4, 18) B (2, 12) C (10, 14)

14 IJK; I (8, 18) J (14, 14) K (15, 19)

15 PQRS; P (5, 12) Q (2, 6) R (10, 8) S (13, 14); use altitudes RT, RU perpendicular to PQ, PS.

16 WXYZ; W (9, 6) X (4, 4) Y (9, 2) Z (14, 4); draw one altitude, also use an exact method.

Start a new page with axes and scales again as before. Answers can be written by the figures.

17 Construct triangle ABC given B (2, 14), C (8, 14), A is above BC, angle ABC = 66.5°, angle ACB = 49°. Write down

(a) the co-ordinates of A,   (b) angle A.   (c) the lengths AB and AC.

18 Draw triangle DEF with D (10, 18), E (10, 13), angle EDF = 40°, angle DEF = 103°; F is on the right of DE. Write down the co-ordinates of F and the sizes of angle F and of DF and EF.

19 KLMN has L (2, 6), M (12, 6), angle L = 68°, angle M = 50°, KL = 4.3cm, MN = 7.8 cm. K and N are above L and M. Construct KLMN and find

(a) co-ordinates of K, N,   (b) angles K, N,   (c) the length of KN.

20 *Submarine patrol.* Start a new page, axes and scales as before. Each cm represents 1 km. A submarine starts at A (2, 14) and travels 12 km eastward to B (14, 14). It then turns 144° clockwise and travels 12 km to C, then turns 144° clockwise again and goes 12 km to D, then does the same turning and travelling two more times. Draw the five journeys carefully.

(a) How far is it from A at the end?

(b) Write down the bearings for the five journeys.

(c) If all the points where the submarine turns were to be visited in some order, beginning and ending at A, what would be the minimum total length of journey required?

Draw and investigate

The following work is best done in an exercise book (or on paper) with $\frac{1}{2}$cm or 1cm squares.

1   Spiral of squares

This takes up most of a page in your book, or half a sheet of A4 squared paper. Mark the point O fairly near the top of the page, with about 5cm clear space above O and about 8cm space to the left of O. Draw the square $OABP$ of side 1cm with OA going east (to the right) and OP north (up). The next square is $OBCQ$ (the side OB being a diagonal of the first square) with OQ going north-west. Then draw $OCDR$ with OR going west, and similarly $ODES, OEFT, OFGU, OGHV$.

Under the figure copy and complete the following, putting fractions or numbers in the gaps:

(a) $\triangle OBP$ is _____ of square $OABP$, and is _____ of square $OBCQ$, so the area of $OBCQ$ is _____ times the area of $OABP$. Likewise $OCDR$'s area is _____ times that of $OBCQ$.

(b) The areas of the seven squares are _____ cm^2, and their sides are the square roots of the areas; they are _____ cm to 3SF. (Calculate the sides; check by measurement.)

2   Journeys round an island

This needs a whole page in your book, or most of a sheet of A4. The island ABC is a triangle, with AB = 12km going from north to south, BC = 9km going from west to east, so there is a right angle at B. The scale is 1cm to 1km, and A should be 3cm from the left-hand margin and 5cm below the top of the page. Draw the island.

Toby and Scott travel round the island, Toby on land, Scott by sea. On the first day Toby goes right round the island on land, always staying 1km away from the coast, while Scott sails round the island, also staying 1km away from the coast. The second day they repeat the process, but travel always 2km from the coast. Draw their journeys carefully; use colour to distinguish sea journeys from land journeys, and from the coast itself.

(a) Toby's journeys are triangles $A_1B_1C_1$ and $A_2B_2C_2$, similar to ABC. Draw the lines AA_1A_2, BB_1B_2 and CC_1C_2. What do these lines do to the angles of the triangle ABC? How far from the coast do they meet, if you produce (i.e. extend) them? This meeting point is the *incentre* of the triangle, the point that is furthest from the coast.

(b) Measure AC; it is a whole number of km. Copy and complete: "The sides of $\triangle ABC$ are in the ratio 9:12: _____ = 3:4: _____ ." Repeat this for the other two triangles. (They should all be whole numbers of km; you can round your measurements to the nearest km.)

(c) Find the total length of each of Scott's sea journeys, explaining your method.

3   Exploring the island

Redraw the same island ABC as in no. 2. This time the whole figure is inside the island, so less space is needed on the page.

Karl starts at K on AB, 2km south of A. He goes east, parallel to BC, till he reaches AC, then parallel to AB till he reaches BC, then parallel to AC till he reaches AB; he is then 2km north of B. He again does three stages parallel to BC, AB and AC respectively, and finds he is back at K. Check this by careful drawing!

Linda follows the same scheme, starting and finishing at L, 4km south of A on AB. Manoj does a complete trip like the others, but finds he only needs three stages.

Show all the round trips, using a different colour for each.

(a) Manoj starts at M on AB. How far is M from A?

(b) Into how many small triangles is the whole island divided by all the lines you have drawn? Express the perimeter and the area of each small triangle as fractions of the perimeter and area of the island.

(c) How many km long is each of the round trips? Are they all the same length?

(d) One of the trips divides the island into four equal small triangles, and another divides it into nine equal small triangles. Whose trips are these?

Exploring triangles

1 Construct triangle *ABC* with each side 6 cm long. Draw the altitudes *AD, BE, CF*. (*AD* is perpendicular to *BC*, *BE* to *AC* and *CF* to *AB*. *D, E, F* are on *BC, AC, AB* respectively.)

(a) Measure the altitudes and express *AD/AB* as a fraction and as a decimal, to 2DP.

(b) The centre of the triangle is *O*. Express *OD* as a simple fraction of *OA* and *OA* as a simple fraction of *AD*.

(c) Measure the angles *BAC, ABC, BCA, BAD* and *BOC*.

2 Redo 1(a), (b) with a triangle in which all sides are 7.5 cm.

3 Construct △*ABC* with *AB* = *AC* = 7.8 cm, *BC* = 6 cm, and mark the midpoints *L, M, N* of *BC, CA, AB* respectively. The figure is not drawn to scale!

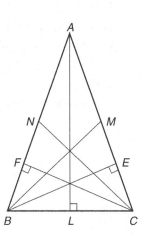

(a) Measure *MN, NL* and *LM*. What do you notice?

(b) *AL, BM* and *CN* meet at *G*. Express as simple fractions *AG/AL* and *GM/BG*.

(c) Draw the altitudes *AL, BE* and *CF* and measure them. How far from A do they meet?

(d) Measure angles *BAC, ABC, BCA* and find their sum.

(e) Try to calculate angles *BAL* and *CBE*; check by measuring them.

(f) Calculate *BC* × *AL* and *AC* × *BE*; try to account for what you notice.

4 (a) (b) Repeat 3 (a), (b) with a triangle *ABC* in which *BC* = 7, *CA* = 6.5, *AB* = 7.5 cm.

(c) Draw and measure the altitudes *AD, BE, CF*. How far from A do they meet?

(d) Measure angles *BAC, ABC, CBA* and find their sum.

(e) Measure angles *BAD* and *BCF*. Try to account for what you notice.

(f) Does what you noticed in 3(f) apply in this triangle?

5 (a) What sort of triangle did you draw in no 1? in no 3? in no 4?

(b) When do all the altitudes bisect (divide into equal halves) the sides?

(c) When does just one altitude bisect a side?

(d) What can you say about the sum of the angles of a triangle? Why?

(e) How is the triangle *LMN* formed by the midpoints related to the original triangle?

6 **Napoleon's theorem**

Draw triangle *ABC* with *BC* = 9, *CA* = 4.8, *AB* = 7.2 cm. Mark on *BC* the points *D, E* which divide *BC* into three equal parts. (They are called points of trisection: *D* is 3 cm and *E* is 6 cm from *B*.) Construct equilateral triangle *DEP* with *P* outside triangle *ABC*. Similarly draw triangles *FGQ, HIR* with *F, G* trisecting *CA* and *H, I* trisecting *AB*, and *Q, R* outside *ABC*, (as in the figure, which is not accurate). Now join the sides of triangle *PQR* and measure them. What do you notice? Try this construction with another triangle with sides of your own choice, and see whether the same thing happens again.

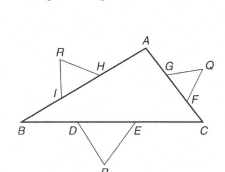

Exploring triangles *(continued)*

7   The three jets

Draw an equilateral triangle *ABC* with each side 12cm. This represents a training area with side 12km. Three jets P, Q, R start at points on *AB*: P at *A*, Q at Q_1, 4km from *A*, R at R_1, 8km from *A*. They all fly at right angles to *BC* until they meet *BC* at P_2, Q_2, R_2 respectively, then at right angles to *AC*, meeting it at P_3, Q_3, R_3, then at right angles to *AB*, reaching it at P_4, Q_4 and R_4. Draw these journeys, using a different colour for each jet.

(a)   Where is Q_4?

(b)   How far apart are P_4, Q_4 and R_4?

(c)   What happens to the distances between jets after each part of the journey? Why?

(d)   If the jets do another complete circuit, how far apart will P_7, Q_7 and R_7 be? (You can try to check this by drawing if you have a steady hand!)

(e)   If another jet starts from somewhere on *AB* and carries out this exercise, whereabouts will it meet the three sides of $\triangle ABC$ on its 10th circuit?

Starting vectors and Pythagoras

Using an A4 sheet of squared paper, with squares of side 1cm, draw axes with origin O near the centre, so that x ranges from -10 to 10, y from -14 to 14.

1 Starting at A, $(0, 9)$, draw the vector $\begin{pmatrix} 1 \\ 3 \end{pmatrix}$, which means going 1 along and 3 up from A, taking you

to $(1, 12)$. From there draw $\begin{pmatrix} 3 \\ -1 \end{pmatrix}$ to take you to $(4, 11)$, then do successively $\begin{pmatrix} -1 \\ -3 \end{pmatrix}$ and $\begin{pmatrix} -3 \\ 1 \end{pmatrix}$.

This gets you back to A. What shape have you made?

Has it a centre? If so, where?

Repeat no.1 with starting points and vectors as follows, in nos. 2 to 5.

2 $B(-9, 10)$ $\begin{pmatrix} 1 \\ 2 \end{pmatrix}\begin{pmatrix} 3 \\ 1 \end{pmatrix}\begin{pmatrix} -1 \\ -2 \end{pmatrix}\begin{pmatrix} -3 \\ -1 \end{pmatrix}$

3 $C(7, 10)$ $\begin{pmatrix} -3 \\ -3 \end{pmatrix}\begin{pmatrix} 6 \\ 0 \end{pmatrix}\begin{pmatrix} -3 \\ 3 \end{pmatrix}$

4 $D(2, 2)$ $\begin{pmatrix} 2 \\ 3 \end{pmatrix}\begin{pmatrix} -2 \\ 1 \end{pmatrix}\begin{pmatrix} -2 \\ -1 \end{pmatrix}\begin{pmatrix} 2 \\ -3 \end{pmatrix}$

5 $E(-3, 5)$ $\begin{pmatrix} -2 \\ 2 \end{pmatrix}\begin{pmatrix} -2 \\ 0 \end{pmatrix}\begin{pmatrix} -2 \\ -2 \end{pmatrix}\begin{pmatrix} 0 \\ -2 \end{pmatrix}\begin{pmatrix} 2 \\ -2 \end{pmatrix}\begin{pmatrix} 2 \\ 0 \end{pmatrix}\begin{pmatrix} 2 \\ 2 \end{pmatrix}\begin{pmatrix} 0 \\ 2 \end{pmatrix}$

6 Starting at F $(-1, -3)$ draw $\begin{pmatrix} 2 \\ -1 \end{pmatrix}$ and follow on with $\begin{pmatrix} 2 \\ 1 \end{pmatrix}$. What two vectors are needed to complete

a parallelogram? Draw them, say what sort of parallelogram it is and where its centre is.

Repeat no. 6 with the following starting points and vectors in nos. 7 to 9.

7 $G(-9, -5)$ $\begin{pmatrix} 2 \\ 2 \end{pmatrix}\begin{pmatrix} 3 \\ -3 \end{pmatrix}$

8 $H(1, -8)$ $\begin{pmatrix} 1 \\ -3 \end{pmatrix}\begin{pmatrix} 4 \\ 4 \end{pmatrix}$

9 $I(-8, -10)$ $\begin{pmatrix} 4 \\ 2 \end{pmatrix}\begin{pmatrix} -1 \\ -2 \end{pmatrix}$

10 Starting at J $(6, 4)$ draw $\begin{pmatrix} 2 \\ -1 \end{pmatrix}$. This is one side of a square. State the vectors for the other sides, draw them and give the co-ordinates of the centre. (There are two sets of answers.)

11 Repeat no.10 starting at K $(9, -3)$ with first vector $\begin{pmatrix} -3 \\ -1 \end{pmatrix}$.

12 (a) If parallelogram $PQRS$ has PQ (the vector from P to Q) $= \begin{pmatrix} 30 \\ 50 \end{pmatrix}$, what is RS?

(b) If in fact $PQRS$ is a square, find QR, SP and PR.

13 Repeat no.12 taking PQ to be $\begin{pmatrix} a \\ b \end{pmatrix}$; again there are two sets of answers.

14 The *position vector* of A is the vector OA from the origin to A, which is $\begin{pmatrix} 0 \\ 9 \end{pmatrix}$; (see no.1.)

Write down the position vectors of C and D, and vectors AC, CA, AD, DA, CD and DC.

15 Write down the vectors   (a) OB, OE, BE, EB (b) OG, OF, FG, GF.

16 If P and Q have position vectors $\mathbf{p}$ and $\mathbf{q}$, express PQ and QP in terms of $\mathbf{p}$ and $\mathbf{q}$.

Starting vectors and Pythagoras *(continued)*

17 The figure shows what you have drawn in no.1, the vectors being the sides of the sloping square. The area of this square can be found by starting with the bigger square with horizontal and vertical sides, which acts as a 'crate' for the sloping square, and subtracting from this the areas of the triangles which are outside the sloping square, like 'packing'. Use this approach to find the area of the sloping square, and hence to find the length of a side of the square, to 3SF. This length is the **magnitude** (i.e. the size) of each of the vectors that you drew in no.1.

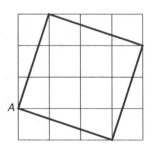

18 Use the 'crate minus packing' method to find the areas of the squares drawn in nos. 10 and 11, and hence to find the magnitudes of the vectors that form the sides.

19 The figure shows a right-angled triangle with sides 12, 5 and *c*, with a sloping square drawn on the hypotenuse *c*. Copy this on squared paper, draw a crate round the sloping square, and use this to find the area of the square and hence to find *c*. Check by measurement.

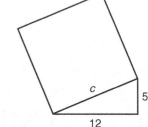

20 Repeat no.18 with triangles of sides

   (a) 3, 4   (b) 3, 2   (c) 2, 2.

21 If the sides containing the right angle are *a* and *b*, what is then the area of the 'crate'? and of the 'packing'? Hence find the area of the sloping square, simplifying the answer as much as possible. What relationship can you deduce between the three sides of any right-angled triangle? Check your result by using it to find again the answers to nos. 19 and 20.

22 In the triangles on the right,

   (a) Find *c* if *a* = 15, *b* = 8,

   (b) Find *w* if *u* = 16, *v* = 12,

   (c) Find *a* if *b* = 2, *c* = 3,

   (d) Find *c* if *b* = 4 and angle *A* = 45°,

   (e) Find *w* and *u* if *v* = 3 and angle *U* = 60°. (Reflect the triangle in the side of length *u* to make a special triangle.)

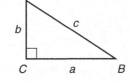

23 If points *P* and *Q* are (*x*, 24) and (15, *y*) and their position vectors both have magnitude 25, find all possible values of *x* and *y*.

24 A goat is tethered by a 41m rope to a post 40m away from a long straight hedge. What length of the hedge can the goat reach?

25 A 10m rod stands vertically against a wall. How far must the bottom be moved away so that the top moves down 1mm? How much further to make it move down another 2mm?

26 A circle with radius 10 has its centre at (3, 2). Draw a sketch of the circle together with the line *x* = 9 and calculate the co-ordinates of the points where the line cuts the circle.

27 Find the lengths of the sides and diagonals of quadrilateral *OPQR* with *P* = (6, 3), *Q* = (5, 5), *R* = (−1, 2). What can you deduce about the quadrilateral?

Parallelograms

1 Construct, on paper or with geometry software, six parallelograms *ABCD* with *BC* = 6 cm in each one, *AB* = 2.5 cm in the 1st, 3rd and 5th, *AB* = 6 cm in the 2nd, 4th and 6th. Make angle *ABC* be 30° in the 1st and 2nd, 60° in the 3rd and 4th, 90° in the 5th and 6th. Join diagonals *AC* and *BD*, meeting at *K*.

   (a) Measure *AK*, *AC*, *BK*, *BD* and the angles *AKD*, *DBC* in each parallelogram.

   (b) Some of the six parallelograms are special types. Identify these and say which type each is.

   (c) When do the diagonals bisect each other? When are they equal in length? When are they perpendicular? When do they bisect the angles of the parallelogram?

2 Use a sheet of graph paper in the portrait position, with origin near the bottom left hand corner, and a scale of millimetres along each axis. Values of *x* are from 0 to 160, and those of *y* from 0 to 200. Construct *ABCD* from the data for each part, with diagonals meeting at *K*. State the coordinates of the corners not given in the question.

   (a) Parallelogram *ABCD* has *B* at (80, 160), *C* at (114, 160), *K* at (104, 178).

   (b) Parallelogram: *B*, *C* at (20, 160), (56, 160). *AC* = 50 mm, *BD* = 58 mm.

   (c) Rectangle: *A* is (20, 144), *B* is (20, 130), *AC* = 50 mm.

   (d) Square: *A* (110, 144), *B* (100, 120). *C* is lower than *B*.

   (e) Rhombus: *A* (40, 100), *K* (40, 90). *AB* = 26 mm.

   (f) Square: *A* (116, 102), *C* (116, 66). *B* is left of *AC*.

   (g) Rectangle: *C* (44, 0), *K* (42, 29). *BC* = 26 mm, *B* is left of *AC*.

   (h) Rhombus: *B* (90, 10), *K* (120, 30). *BA* produced passes through (134, 74).

3 Prepare another page of graph paper with origin and axes as in no. 2.

   (a) *P* (76, 160), *Q* (108, 170) and *R* (80, 180) are three vertices of a parallelogram. Construct the three possible positions for the fourth vertex, and give their coordinates. If they are *X*, *Y* and *Z*, what can you say about the positions of *P*, *Q* and *R* in relation to the sides of △*XYZ*?

   (b) Repeat (a) with *P* (70, 130), *Q* (50, 150) and *R* (40, 140).

   (c) Triangle *ABC* has *D*, *E* and *F* as midpoints of *BC*, *CA* and *AB* respectively. Given the positions *D* (30, 66), *E* (44, 100) and *F* (20, 90), find *A*, *B* and *C*.

   (d) Repeat (c) given *E* (100, 80), *F* (120, 80), *AB* = *AC* and *A* is 60 mm below *BC*.

   (e) Repeat (c) given *E* (90, 35), *F* (50, 35), ∠*B* = 90°, *AC* = 100 mm, *A* is above *BC*.

4 **True or false?**

   Which of the statements (a) to (l) are true? Which are false? Begin with each by trying to show it is false, by drawing a figure that demonstrates this, (a counter-example.)

   For instance, the statement

   "Every quadrilateral with at least two right angles must be a rectangle"

   can be disproved by drawing a quadrilateral with angles 90°, 90°, 50° and 130°. (It cannot be disproved by drawing a square, because a square is a special sort of rectangle.) If you fail to produce a counter-example, the statement may be true; then see if you can prove this.

   (a) A quadrilateral with equal diagonals must be a rectangle.

   (b) A parallelogram with equal diagonals must be a rectangle.

   (c) A quadrilateral with perpendicular diagonals must be a rhombus.

Parallelograms (continued)

    (d) A parallelogram with perpendicular diagonals must be a rhombus.

    (e) A quadrilateral whose diagonals bisect each other must be a parallelogram.

    (f) In $ABCD$, if $AB = CD$ and $AD \| BC$, then $ABCD$ must be a parallelogram.

    (g) If $AB = CD$ and $AB \| CD$ then $ABCD$ must be a parallelogram.

    (h) If both diagonals of a quadrilateral bisect the angles it must be a rhombus.

    (i) If $AB = CD$ and $\angle A = \angle C$, $ABCD$ must be a parallelogram.

    (j) If AC bisects $\angle BAD$ and $\angle BCD$, then

        (1) $BD \perp AC$,

        (2) $ABCD$ must be a rhombus.

    (k) A quadrilateral with both pairs of opposite sides equal must be a parallelogram.

    (l) A quadrilateral with both pairs of opposite angles equal must be a parallelogram.

5   In the rhombus $ABCD$ with centre K,

    (a) If $\angle ABK = 36°$ find $\angle KCD$.

    (b) If $\angle BAD = 126°$ find $\angle KBC$.

    (c) Find $\angle BAD$ given that it is eight times as big as $\angle CDK$.

6 $ABCD$ is a square with centre K. Q is on AB, and $AQ = AK$. Find $\angle AQK$ and $\angle QKB$.

7 ABX is an equilateral triangle within a square $ABCD$. Find $\angle DXC$.

8 $ABCDE$ is a regular pentagon and $CDEP$ is a parallelogram inside it. Draw an accurate figure, taking 4 cm for the length of AB, and

    (a) Calculate angles PEA and APE,

    (b) Prove that CPA is a straight line,

    (c) Prove that DE is perpendicular to CE.

9   Using ruler and compass only, construct a regular hexagon $ABCDEF$ inscribed in a circle of radius 5 cm with centre O.

    (a) By considering AD and CF, or otherwise, show that $ACDF$ is a rectangle.

    (b) By considering the quadrilateral $ODEF$, or otherwise, show that $OE \perp DF$.

10 $ABPQ$ and $ACXY$ are squares lying outside $\triangle ABC$, which is right-angled at A.

    Prove that PAX is a straight line.

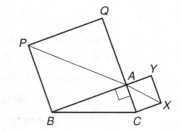

11   Given a triangle ABC with a right angle at B, show how to construct accurately a square with one corner at B and the other corners on BC, CA and AB respectively. Use your method to construct the square when $AB = 12$ cm, $BC = 6$ cm, and measure the side of the square.

© tarquin publications

Regular polygons

The first six questions are about a regular hexagon drawn in a circle of radius 6 cm with centre O, as in the figure.

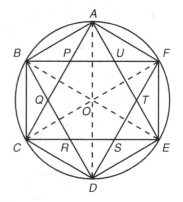

1 Calculate

(a) $\angle AOB$ (b) $\angle OAB$

(c) AB. Now draw the hexagon full size, starting with A and stepping round the circle with your compass to mark the other vertices B, C, D, E, F. Draw the sides and diagonals. You can use colour, a different colour for each different length.

2 Calculate

(a) $\angle ABC$ (b) $\angle BAC$ (c) $\angle OAC$ (d) $\angle APB$.

3 (a) Measure the shorter diagonal AC and check that $AC \approx \frac{26}{15} \times AB$.

(b) Parts of the shorter diagonals form the hexagon $PQRSTU$. Explain why PQ has to be a simple fraction of AC, and express PQ as a fraction of AB.

4 What can you say about the areas of

(a) $\triangle OPU$ and $\triangle APU$,   (b) $\triangle ABP$ and $\triangle APU$? Why?

(c) Hence express the area of $PQRSTU$ as a fraction of $ABCDEF$ by considering each as made up of a number of triangles, all having the same area.

(d) The area fraction you have found in (c) should be the square of the fraction PQ/AB that you found in 5(b). Check whether this is exactly so. If it is not, which fraction is actually correct? Why?

5 How would you cut up the hexagon into three pieces that could make a rhombus?

6 Draw a regular octagon with side 3.4 cm, as in the diagram. Produce four sides to make the square $PQRS$. Measure PA and hence calculate an estimate of the area of the octagon.

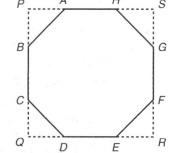

7 Join AC and AD. Calculate

(a) $\angle ABC$ (b) $\angle BAC$ (c) $\angle DAB$ (d) $\angle DAH$.

8 (a) Draw the other diagonals from A. What angle does each make with the next?

Find the angles between

(b) BH and AE (c) BH and AC

9 Colour in all the diagonals, using a different colour for each different length.

How many regular octagons can you find inside $ABCDEFGH$?

10 Draw a regular pentagon $ABCDE$ of side 55mm. Join the diagonals. They form a five-pointed star whose 'nucleus' is pentagon $FGHIJ$; the 'flames' are triangles like AIH, and the length of a side AI is called the *flame length*. Now

(a) state the size of $\angle ABC$ and use this to calculate $\angle BAC$ by considering triangle BAC.

(b) Hence state the size of $\angle HAE$ and calculate $\angle IAH$.

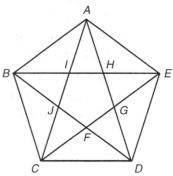

Regular polygons (continued)

11 Call *ABCDE* P1, *FGHIJ* P2. Draw diagonals of P2 to make P3 and its flames, then diagonals of P3 and so on until the pentagon is too small to continue. Measure sides, diagonals and flame lengths of P1–P4 and copy and complete the table

Pentagon	Side/mm	Diagonal/mm	Flame Length/mm
P1	55	89	?
P2			

    (a) What do you notice about diagonals and flame lengths? Why does this happen? (consider e.g. *AI* and *IG*). Hence state the flame length of P1.

    (b) Add the side and flame length for each pentagon and explain what you notice by considering $\triangle ABH$.

12 (a) Using the results of no.12, calculate to 4DP the ratio diagonal/side for P1, P2 and P3. Why are the answers close to each other, and why are they not exactly equal?

    (b) Let the true ratio diagonal/side = *t*. Thus in P2 *IG* = *tIH*, so *AI* also = *tIH*. By considering $\triangle$s *ABH* and *AIH* explain why *AB* = *tAH*, and deduce that $AB = t^2 IH$.

    (c) Explain why *BH* = (*t* + 1)*IH*, and deduce that t must satisfy $t^2 = t + 1$.

    (d) Use trial and a calculator to find *t* to 4DP. This number is called the *golden ratio*.

    (e) Calculate to 4DP the ratio side/diagonal for P1 – P3. How do the answers compare with those for part (a)? Explain this by using the equation you found in (c).

13 Kürschak's tile. Draw a square of side 12cm with centre *O* on one of the printed lines in your book. Draw a circle centre *O* to touch the four sides of the square and draw 6 diameters of the circle making angles 0°, 30°, 60°, 90°, 120° and 150° with the horizontal. The end points of these are the vertices of a regular dodecagon (12-sided polygon.) Draw the sides of the dodecagon.

    (a) On each of the 12 sides construct an equilateral triangle pointing in towards *O*. Join the innermost vertex of each triangle to *O*. As well as the twelve equilateral triangles there are now some isosceles triangles inside the dodecagon. How big are their angles? How long is the longest side of each? How many of them are there?

    (b) Join each corner of the square to the two nearest vertices of the dodecagon. What sorts of triangles does this make, and how many of each sort?

    (c) Use the triangles to find what fraction of the square is inside the dodecagon, and hence calculate the area of the dodecagon.

    (d) If the square had side 2*r*, so that the circle's radius was *r*, what would the area of the dodecagon be? Use your answer to show that π must be a little greater than 3.

    (e) Colour the figure suitably and describe what it is about.

    (This tile was invented by J. Kürschak about 1898; it is described in the October 1978 *Mathematical Gazette*, which gives the original reference.)

Enemy Territory

You will need a sheet of graph paper in the 'portrait' position, the origin being near the bottom left hand corner (at an intersection of two heavy lines) and the axes marked 0, 2, 4, 6 etc. The scale is 2cm to 2km. Values of x (easting) go up to 14; values of y up to 20.

The sheet represents the map of a piece of enemy territory about which you are finding information. You are in charge of six agents who have infiltrated the area and established themselves at the following places:

A   (2, 6) (i.e. 2km east and 6km north of the origin)   C   (12, 14)   E   (13, 19) and

B   (8, 6)   D   (6, 14)   F   (2, 2).

Mark these on your map and *check carefully* that you have done this correctly: e.g. check that B and C are 6km east of A and D respectively, and F is 4km south of A.

As a further check, and to revise bearings, find the distance and bearing of

1   D from A

2   C from E.

Write the answers to these and the other questions in the 2cm strip at the right hand edge of the map, (from 14 to 16km east of O) or in your book.

Now locate and give the co-ordinates of the following features from the information given by your agents. In some cases there are two possible positions: then give both.

3   A granary G is on a bearing of 26.5° from A, and 315° from B.

4   A heliport H is on a bearing 166° from B, and 194° from C.

5   The secret internal telecommunications centre I is 5.1km from B, 5.8km from C.

6   An important railway junction J is on 300° from C and is 4km from D.

7   A missile launcher M is also on 300° from C and is 7km from D.

8   A nuclear reactor has been built at N, which is equidistant from A and B, (that means the distances AN and BN are equal) and is on the same bearing from C as it is from D.

9   The country's other main source of energy is the power station P, which is equidistant from C and D, and is 2.6km from B.

10   Surveillance against enemy aircraft and missiles is done by the radar station at R, equidistant from A and D, and due north of A.

11   The army's central supply depôt S is also equidistant from A and D, and is 2.6km north of the straight road joining A and B.

12   The railway's main terminus T is equidistant from B, C and D.

13   A and F are on the bank of a straight canal which is used by a water pumping station W that supplies the needs of the area. W is equidistant from the canal and the road AB, and is south-west of C.

14   The agent at E has been asked to recommend a strategic point X for landing paratroops. He recommends that X should be equidistant from CD and CE, and as close to E as possible.

15   After receiving and processing the data, you radio your agent at A (in code) to ask for further information, which you need to remove the uncertainties about some of the locations. He apologizes and tells you that J is nearly equidistant from I and T, and that the bearings of P and N from I differ by just over 180°. What do you deduce?

Reflections

1 (a) Draw the image when the face F_1 is reflected in the line AB. Label the image F_2 and write the co-ordinates of the tip of F_2's nose in your exercise book.

   (b) Draw F_3, the image when F_1 is reflected in CD, and write co-ordinates of nose tip.

   (c) In what way are F_2 and F_3 like each other and different from F_1? What sort of movement could map F_2 into F_3?

   (d) Draw F_4, the image of F_1 in BD, and F_5, the image of F_4 in CD. Write nose tip co-ordinates.

   (e) Is F_4 more like F_1 or F_2? What about F_5?

   (f) What simple movement could map F_1 into F_5? Could a reflection do it?

   (g) Draw the image of F_6 of F_1 in AE and write down the co-ordinates of the nose tip.

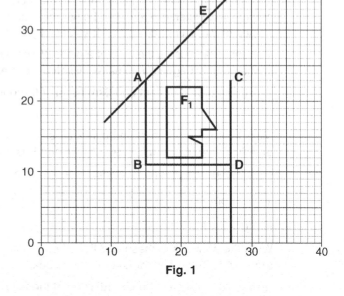

Fig. 1

2 Draw the reflections in AH of the lines in Fig.2. Write down the co-ordinates of the images of B, C, D, E, F, G.

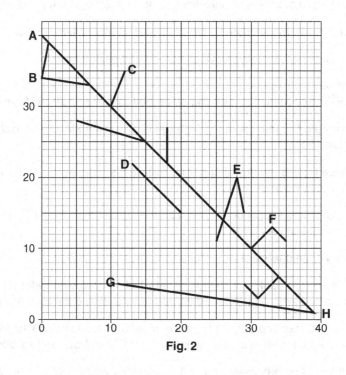

Fig. 2

Reflections *(continued)*

3   In Fig.3,

(a)   what happens if rectangle ABCD is reflected in PR?

(b)   Does any other reflection produce a similar result?

(c)   Draw the reflection of ABCD in BD and write down co-ordinates of the images of A and C.

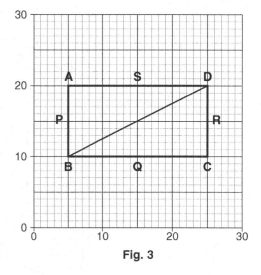

Fig. 3

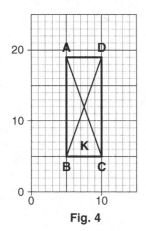

Fig. 4

4   (a)   Draw the reflections K_1 and K_2 of the rectangle K in AC, BD respectively (Fig.4) and give co-ordinates of the most eastward corner of each.

(b)   What single movement could map K_1 into K_2? (There are several answers to this; give all you can.)

5   Draw all lines of symmetry (if any) for each of the shapes in Figure 5, and write down how many there are.

     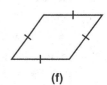

    (a)   **(b)**   **(c)**   **(d)**   **(e)**   **(f)**   **(g)**

Further reflections

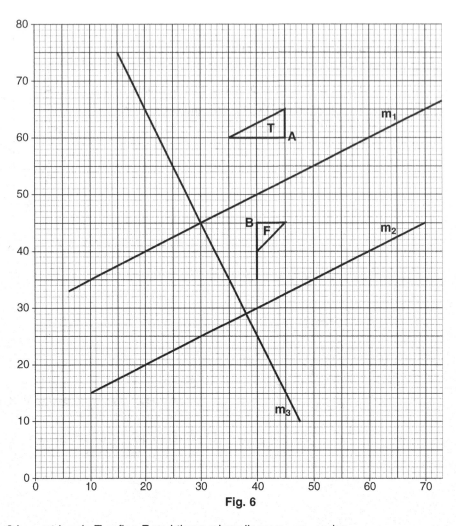

Fig. 6

6   Figure 6 has a triangle T, a flag F and three mirror lines m_1, m_2 and m_3.

   (a)   Reflect T in m_1, label the image M_1T and write down the co-ordinates of M_1A the image of A. Reflect M_1T in m_2, label the image M_2M_1T and write co-ordinates of M_2M_1A. How is M_2M_1T related to T? In other words, what single movement takes T to M_2M_1T? Describe this movement as precisely as you can.

   (b)   Repeat (a) using F and B instead of T and A.

   (c)   What is the shortest movement that takes m_1 to m_2? What connection is there between this and the last parts of (a) and (b)?

   (d)   In no.1, what is the result of reflecting F_2 in AB and then in CD? What single movement has the same effect? How is this related to the shortest movement that takes AB to CD? What can you say about the overall effect of successive reflections in two parallel mirrors?

   (e)   Reflect M_1T in m_3 and write down co-ordinates of M_3M_1A. What simple movement takes T to M_3M_1T? Describe it as precisely as you can.

   (f)   Repeat (e) with F and B. What can you say about the effect of two successive reflections in two perpendicular mirrors? Which part of no.1 confirms this?

   (g)   Draw M_3T and M_3F. Where are M_1M_3T and M_1M_3F? What can you say about M_1M_3?

   (h)   Draw M_2F and M_1M_2F. How is M_1M_2 related to M_2M_1?

Calculating π

The diagram shows an arc of a circle of radius 3 m; the chord AB and the two radii make an equilateral triangle of side 3 m. Six of these triangles would fit together to make a regular hexagon, and six arcs would make a complete circle, with circumference $2\pi r = 6\pi$; so the length of the arc shown is just π m. We will be calculating successive approximations to the length of the arc.

Initially we have the chord AB = 3m, and we take this as π_0, our starting approximation.

I have drawn OP1M1 at right angles to AB.

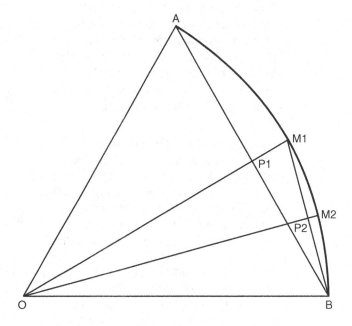

1   Use Pythagoras's theorem, plus the fact that P1 is the midpoint of AB, to calculate P1B, OP1, then P1M1, then M1B. Our next approximation π_1 is then 2M1B, which is nearer the arc length than AB. Keep all lengths to full precision in your calculator, or else write down all the decimal digits each time, so that accuracy is not lost in the process.

2   Repeat the processes in no.1 to find P2B, OP2, P2M2, M2B and then π_2 = 4M2B.

3   Continue finding further approximations to π, either with your calculator or by setting up a sheet in Excel, as in the screenshot below. One column will be for PB (i.e. P1B, then P2B, then P3B etc.) Other columns will be for OP, PM, MB and approximations to π. You will also want a column to contain the powers of 2 (2, 4, 8 etc) that are used to convert MB to π. After you have completed the second row, you should be able to continue by replicating down. See how far you can go before there is no longer any improvement in accuracy.

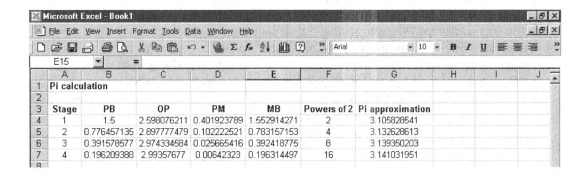

Similar shapes

1   The original hammer picture has been transformed to give the versions (a) to (e).The transformations used have been either **enlargement**, increasing all dimensions in the same ratio, or **stretches** by different factors in the horizontal and vertical directions, resulting in a change of shape. Some pictures have also been rotated.

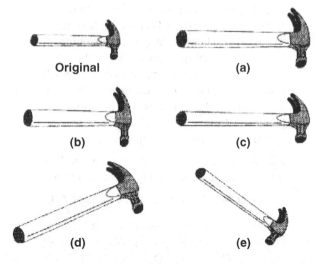

Original   (a)

(b)   (c)

(d)   (e)

Measure the length and the width of each hammer, and any relevant angles, and hence give full details of the transformations that have made each of (a) to (e). Which of them are geometrically similar to the original picture? Are any that are not similar to the original similar to each other?

2   Looking at the versions (a) to (f) of the original aeroplane picture, try to judge by eye which of them are geometrically similar to the original, which are too fat and which are too slim. Then use measurements of lengths, heights and appropriate angles to find precisely what transformations have been used to make each of (a) to (f), and hence to check your original assessments. Is there a pair similar to each other but not to the original?

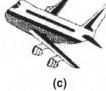

Original   (a)

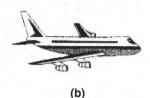

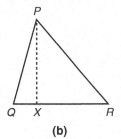

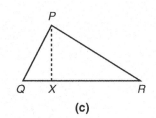

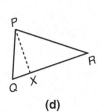

(b)   (c)   (d)   (e)   (f)

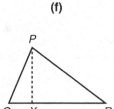

3   The original triangle *PQR* with altitude *PX* perpendicular to *QR* has been transformed by enlargement or by horizontal and/or vertical stretching, followed in one case by rotation. Measure the sides, altitude and angles of each triangle, and state what transformations have been applied to make each of (a) to (d) from the original.

(e) In which cases are all the angles unchanged?

(f) In which cases are all the sides of the transformed triangle changed in the same ratio?

(a)   (b)   (c)   (d)

Similar shapes *(continued)*

4   Two figures are similar provided (1) corresponding angles are equal, and (2) corresponding sides are in proportion.

   (a)   Can two triangles with corresponding angles equal have sides *not* in proportion? Explain.

   (b)   Sketch two quadrilaterals that satisfy (1) but not (2), and two that satisfy (2) but not (1).

5   A tree's shadow is 140 foot long when a 5 foot boy casts a $17\frac{1}{2}$ foot shadow. Find the height of the tree.

6   A fence of height 2m is 3m away from a wall parallel to the fence. A ladder leans against the wall and just touches the top of the fence, while the bottom of the ladder is 50cm away from the fence. Draw a sketch, identify two similar triangles and find how far up the wall the ladder reaches.

7   (a)   A cone of height 36cm and base radius 8cm has the top 24cm cut off. What is the radius of the cut surface? What height would have been cut off to leave a cut surface with radius 5cm?

   (b)   A pyramid has a square base of side 40m. The top part is cut off, leaving a horizontal top surface which is a square of side 24m, at a height of 18m above the base. How high was the whole pyramid?

8   The sun, 93 000 000 miles from the earth, looks the same size as the moon, 240 000 miles away. If the moon's diameter is $\frac{1}{4}$ of the earth's, how many earth diameters would equal the sun's diameter?

9   The triangle *ABC*, right-angled at *A*, has an altitude *AD* drawn.

   The lengths of *BC*, *CA* and *AB* are *a*, *b* and *c*; $a = x + y$.

   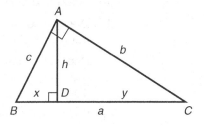

   (a)   Name three similar triangles in the figure, with vertices in corresponding order.

   (b)   Show that $h/x = y/h$, and find *h* if *x* = 8cm, *y* = 18cm.

   (c)   Show that $h = bc/a$, and find the altitudes of a right-angled triangle with sides 7, 24 and 25 m.

   (d)   Show that $x = c^2/a$, $y = b^2/a$, and deduce Pythagoras's theorem.

10   The rectangle *ABCD* has *AB* = 20cm. *M* is the mid-point of *BC* and *K* is the mid-point of *BM*.

   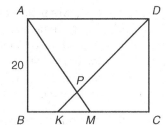

   (a)   Find the height of triangle *PKM*, taking *KM* as base.

   (b)   Express the areas of triangles *PKM* and *APD* as fractions of the area of the whole rectangle.

11   A ray of light from *A* is reflected by the mirror *MN* at *P* and passes through *B*. The law of reflection states that $\angle APM = \angle BPN$.

   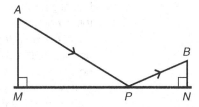

   (a)   If *AM* = 8cm, *BN* = 6cm and *MN* = 35cm, find *MP*.

   (b)   If *AM* = 85cm, *BN* = 15cm and the direct distance *AB* = 250cm, find *MN* and find the total distance travelled by the ray.

   (c)   By considering the reflection *B'* of *B* in the mirror, prove that, if *Q* is some point on *MN* other than *P*, then *AQ* + *QB* > *AP* + *PB*. (Draw *QB'*.)

12   A *golden rectangle* is one whose length and width are in such a ratio that, if a square is cut off with side equal to the width, the remainder of the rectangle is similar to the original. Show that, if the ratio of length to width is *x*:1, then $x^2 = x + 1$. Using trial, or otherwise, find *x* correct to 4DP.

Locus: Where are the points?

1 Describe as fully as you can, with a sketch where helpful, the locus of

   (a) a door handle when the door is swung open through 90°,

   (b) a child's head as the child slides down a straight chute into a swimming pool,

   (c) the centre of a penny that rolls round another penny that lies at rest on a table.

   (d) a piece of grit picked up by the tread of a car tyre, as the car continues to move on.

2 Mark two points A and B 6cm apart, with AB sloping at about 30° to the horizontal.

   (a) Where are the points that are 5cm away from A? Draw the locus of these points.

   (b) Mark the two points which are 5cm from A and 5cm from B. How far are they from each other?

   (c) Locate similarly the points P for which $PA = PB = 4$cm, then those for which $PA = PB = 3$cm, then 6cm, then 7cm.

      Hence draw the locus of points P for which $PA = PB$. Is the locus a straight line? What angle does it make with AB? Where does it meet AB?

   (d) If a point moves so as to be equidistant from two given points, what is its locus?

3 Draw two long lines l and m crossing at the centre of a page, with l horizontal and m at 60° to l.

   (a) Where are the points that are 1cm away from l? Draw the locus and describe it.

   (b) Draw the locus of points that are 1cm away from m; mark the points that are 1cm from l and from m. How many are there?

   (c) Repeat the drawing in (a) and (b) for distances of 2, 3, 4, 5 and 6 cm, marking in each case the points that are the specified distance from l and from m. Then draw the locus of P such that P is the same distance from l as from m. What angles do the parts of the locus make with l?

   (d) What is the locus of a point which stays equidistant from two given intersecting straight lines?

   (e) What would the locus in (d) be if the two given lines were parallel?

4 A square plate $ABCD$ with side 3cm rests in a vertical position on a horizontal table, with A and B on the table, B to the right of A. It is rotated about B until C is on the table, then about C until D is on the table, then about D until A is back on the table. Make a sketch and then an accurate drawing of the locus of A, and calculate the length of the locus.

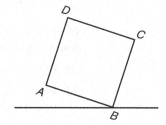

5 Given two points A and B with $AB = 8$cm,

   (a) Investigate the locus of points P such that the angle APB is 90°. Do this by putting a right angle corner of a piece of paper onto your book in such a way that two of the edges go through A and B. Mark the position of the corner, then move the paper so that the corner P is in a new position, but with two edges of the paper still going through A and B. Keep marking positions of P in this way, then try to join them up with a curve, and describe the curve as fully as possible.

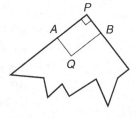

   Can you explain why this particular curve is the locus? (Consider the diagonals of the rectangle $PAQB$ shown in the figure.)

   (b) Describe and draw the locus of points P such that the area of triangle PAB is 9.6cm^2.

   (c) How many points P are there such that angle APB is 90° and triangle PAB has area 9.6cm^2? How far are these points from A and B? Answer by measurement and, if you can, by calculation.

Locus: Where are the points? *(continued)*

For questions 6 to 9 use a new page of squared paper or graph paper, make the origin at or near the centre so that *x* ranges from –8 to 8 and *y* from –10 to 10, the units being cm. Let *O* be (0, 0), *A* be (6, 0), *B* be (6, 4) and *C* be (4, 8).

6 Where are the points equidistant from

    (a) *O* and *A*? (Give the equation of the line you draw; it may help to write down the co-ordinates of some of the points on the line. The same applies to (b) and (d), and in questions 7 and 8.)

    (b) *A* and *B*?

    (c) *O*, *A* and *B*? (Give co-ordinates.)

    (d) *B* and *C*?

    (e) *A*, *B* and *C*?

7 Where are the points which are equidistant from

    (a) the axes of *x* and *y*?

    (b) *AO* produced (that means extended) and *AB* produced?

8 Where does *P* lie if

    (a) ΔOAP (triangle *OAP*) has area 9cm^2?

    (b) ΔPAB has area 2cm^2?

    (c) ΔOAP has area 9cm^2 and ΔPAB has area 2cm^2?

9 (a) Given points *D* (–6, –6) and *E* (0, –6), draw the locus of points *P* such that angle *DPE* = 90°. Hence locate and give co-ordinates of the points *P* such that angle *DPE* = 90° and

    (b) *P* is equidistant from the *x* and *y* axes,

    (c) ΔOAP has area 12 cm^2. (*Challenge: try to calculate the co-ordinates for these to 3DP.)

10 A ladder 10m long is placed vertically against a wall with its foot at *O* where the wall meets the ground, then the foot is pulled away so that the top slides down the wall till the ladder is horizontal.

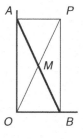

    (a) Draw lots of positions of the ladder and mark in each the mid-point *M* and the point *Q* that is 2.5m from the foot of the ladder. Draw the loci of *M* and *Q*.

    (b) Describe the locus of *M* fully, and try to explain why it has the particular form that it does. (Think of the ladder *AB* in one of its sloping positions as a diagonal of a rectangle *AOBP*; what do you know about the diagonals?)

    (c)* Taking axes through *O*, when *M* has co-ordinates (4, 3) what are the co-ordinates of *Q*? How are the co-ordinates of *Q* found from those of *M*? What transformations done to the locus of *M* will give the locus of *Q*?

11 Use a new page and draw a horizontal line at the bottom to represent a canal which is used for irrigating part of the region represented by the page. The scale is 1cm to 1km. There is also a well, which is 3km north of the mid-point of the canal. The well is used to irrigate those parts that are nearer to the well than to the canal. Draw the boundary between the two parts, consisting of points whose distance from the well equals their distance from the canal. What is the name of the curve formed by these points?

Exotic locations – Loci with Cabri II

Log on and enter Cabri II. Below the menu bar is the button bar which provides most of the operations in Cabri. Each button has several functions, which are listed when you press and hold the button. You then move the mouse down to the option you want. The picture on the button changes to symbolise the chosen activity. Next time you want to use that button for the same activity, just click on the button. For reference I will number and name the buttons as follows:

0   Pointer

1	Point	2	Line	3	Curve
4	Construct	5	Transform	6	Macros
7	Check properties	8	Measure and calculate		
9	Label, trace etc	10	Change appearance.		

1   Bicycle

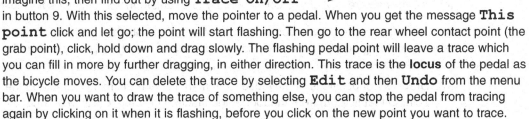

On the menu bar at the top click on **File**, then **Open**. Double click on the **Figures** folder, then choose **Bicycle. fig**. Click, hold and drag the point where the rear wheel touches the ground (where it says "Grab this point.") Notice how the spokes and pedals move.

(a) What shape is the path traced out by a pedal? Try to imagine this, then find out by using **Trace On/Off** in button 9. With this selected, move the pointer to a pedal. When you get the message **This point** click and let go; the point will start flashing. Then go to the rear wheel contact point (the grab point), click, hold down and drag slowly. The flashing pedal point will leave a trace which you can fill in more by further dragging, in either direction. This trace is the **locus** of the pedal as the bicycle moves. You can delete the trace by selecting **Edit** and then **Undo** from the menu bar. When you want to draw the trace of something else, you can stop the pedal from tracing again by clicking on it when it is flashing, before you click on the new point you want to trace.

Find similarly the locus of

(a) the end of a handlebar (this is easy to predict)

(b) the end of a spoke in a wheel. This is called a *cycloid*, and has a *cusp* (a sharp corner) where the end of the spoke meets the ground and is momentarily at rest.

(c) Sketch in your book the loci you have found, labelling each.

2   Bicycle continued

Delete the loci you have traced, and draw a line (*not* a line segment) going through the centre of the rear wheel and through the end of one spoke. (Use button 2 **Lines** and click when you get the message **By this point** at the centre, and again at the end of the spoke. The line you get will include two spokes but will go indefinitely in both directions.) Use button 1 with **Point on object** selected to create a point on the line you have just made. Use **Label** in button 9 to call this point P.

(a) Click on P and drag it till it is a little outside the wheel itself. Make the trace of P as the bicycle moves. You should observe from this that there are times when P is moving backwards while the bicycle is moving forward. This is true of the rim of the flange of the wheel on a train; the rim is further from the axle than the rail itself is, and the bottom of the rim moves backward while the train is speeding forward at 120mph.

(b) Delete the trace locus you have made, select **Trace On/Off** again and click on the flashing point P; this switches Trace off and enables you to move around without a trace.

Now go to button 4 Construct and choose **Locus**, then click on P, then on the grab point; this will draw the locus of P instantaneously. The locus will probably be rather incomplete. To improve it, click on **Options** in the menu bar, then on **Preferences**, then on **Loci Options**; then **change Number of objects in locus** from 50 to 500, then redo the locus. Now click and hold P and move it towards the wheel, and watch how the locus changes as P is moved.

(c) Move P to the edge of a spoke, so that its locus is a cycloid as in 1(c). Make sure **Locus** is selected and move close to the spoke that has P at one end. Click when you get the prompt **This segment**, then click on the grab point to get the *envelope* of the spoke. How is this related to the locus of P?

(d) Sketch the loci you have observed in (a) and (b). What is the locus of P when P is at the centre of the wheel?

3   Sliding ladder

(a) Start by making a horizontal line about halfway up the screen, to represent the ground, with a marked point O on it at about the centre of the screen. Select **Perpendicular line** in button 4 to make a vertical line to represent the wall, going through O. Make a separate segment DE, with length about a quarter of the height of the screen, to represent the length of the ladder. To make the ladder, start by using **Point on object** in button 1 to make a point A on the wall. Use **Compass** in button 4 to draw a circle with centre A and radius DE, then use **Intersection Point** to make the points where the circle meets the ground. Label one of these B, make the segment AB, then drag A and check that AB 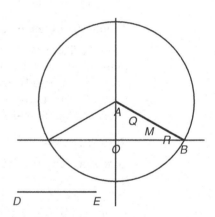 stays a constant length as the ladder moves with A on the wall and B on the ground. The figure shows what you should have, together with the points mentioned below, and also shows the reflection of AB in the wall. You can change the length of the ladder by dragging D or E.

(b) Construct the midpoint M of AB and the midpoints Q, R of AM and MB, and use **Trace** to make their loci as A moves. You can drag A below ground level to get more of each locus, and you can use button 5 to reflect AB, M, Q and R in the wall and trace the reflections as well for completeness.

(c) Make a point P on AB, use **Locus** instead of **Trace** to make the locus of P, then observe how it changes when P is dragged between A and B.

(d) Use **Locus** to make the envelope of the ladder as it slides. Together with the envelope of the reflection of AB this makes a curve called an *astroid*.

(e) Sketch the loci in (b) and the envelope in (d). Try to explain why the locus of M is part of a circle. (Hint: Complete the rectangle AOBC and consider where its diagonals meet, and what you know about a rectangle's diagonals.) The loci of Q and R are parts of *ellipses*, i.e. circles which have been stretched.

More exotic locations

4 Ellipse/hyperbola

From the Figures folder where you got Bicycle, load
Ellipse or hyperbola, which will look like this
diagram. Drag P along AB, and the circles will change.
They are centred on S and T, and have radii made equal to
AP and PB respectively. With P between A and B, the total
of the two radii is constant, so the points Q and R where the
circles meet satisfy SQ + QT = SR + RT = AB = constant.

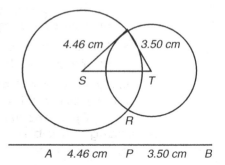

(a) Find the loci of Q and R, using **Trace** or **Locus**.
Together they make an ellipse, with S and T as the
foci. (Gardeners use this approach with a loop of
string round two pegs to mark out elliptical flower
beds.) The path of a planet is nearly an ellipse, with
the sun at one focus.

(b) Drag B to the left until AB is shorter than ST, then find again the loci of Q and R. This time the
two circles will not intersect until P is outside the segment AB, which means that the *difference* of
AP and PB is constant instead of the sum. The loci have two branches and make a *hyperbola*; a
comet passing near the sun but not coming into orbit moves along one branch of a hyperbola.

5 Touching circles locus

Load the figure with this name. As you drag the point P, the moving blue circle always touches the
green circle (i.e. they meet but do not intersect) and always passes through the point S. (To see
how, you can use **Hide/show** in button 10 to reveal the construction lines.) Trace the locus of the
centre Q, then move S outside the green circle and trace the locus of Q again. The circles still touch,
but watch the drama! Sketch and describe the loci. How do they relate to no.4?

6 Parabola locus

Load **Parabola locus 2** and trace the locus of Q, which moves so as to be equidistant from
the focus S and the green horizontal line called the *directrix*. (This takes the place of the green circle
in no.5, and can be viewed as a circle of infinite radius.) See what happens if you change the
position of S. Also trace the envelope of the sloping line through Q (the perpendicular bisector of
SP.) The parabola has only one branch and one focus, and is intermediate between the ellipse and
the hyperbola. It is the shape of the graph of $y = x^2$, and is used in the design of reflectors for lamps
and radio telescopes.

Scaling up and down

1 Four cubes have sides 1cm, 5cm, 20cm and x cm respectively. Find the ratios $S_1 : S_2 : S_3 : S_4$ of their surface areas, and the ratio $V_1 : V_2 : V_3 : V_4$ of their volumes, giving each ratio in its simplest form.

2 Four similar cylinders have base radii 1cm, 2cm, 3cm and x cm respectively. The first has height 5cm. Find the heights h_2 to h_4, the curved surface areas S_1 to S_4 and the volumes V_1 to V_4, leaving π as a letter where relevant. Find in simplest possible form the ratios $h_1 : h_2 : h_3 : h_4$, $S_1 : S_2 : S_3 : S_4$ and $V_1 : V_2 : V_3 : V_4$.

3 Three similar isosceles triangles have bases 6, 12 and 18 cm respectively. The first has height 4cm. Find their perimeters p_1 to p_3 and areas A_1 to A_3 and express the ratios $p_1 : p_2 : p_3$ and $A_1 : A_2 : A_3$ in simplest possible form.

4 If two geometrically similar objects have lengths in the ratio $m : n$, what is the ratio of

(a) their surface areas,

(b) their volumes?

5 Giving each answer as a power of 10, express

(a) 1m² in mm², (c) 1cm² in m², (e) 10^{-9} km² in cm².

(b) 1m³ in mm³, (d) 10^{12} mm³ in km³,

6 The plans for a new boarding-house have been drawn to a scale of 1:200. If a model is made to this scale, find

(a) the area in m² of a corridor whose model area is 3cm²,

(b) the volume in the model of a dormitory that in the real building will have a volume of 36m³.

7 A square whose diagonal is 6cm long has perimeter $12\sqrt{2}$ cm and area 18cm². Find, by scaling, the perimeter and area if the diagonal length is

(a) 1cm

(b) d cm.

8 An equilateral triangle of height 3cm has perimeter $6\sqrt{3}$ cm, area $3\sqrt{3}$ cm². Find the perimeter and area of an equilateral triangle with height h cm.

9 A regular octagon of side 4cm has area 77.25cm². Use this to find the area if the side is a cm.

10 A regular tetrahedron (pyramid on a triangular base) of side 5cm has height $h = 3.06$cm, surface area $A = 43.3$cm² and volume $V = 14.75$cm³. Find h, A and V for a regular tetrahedron with side

(a) 10cm

(b) x cm.

11 The measurements of two tubs of sunflower margarine are as follows:

Mass/g	Length/mm	Width/mm	Height/mm
250	130	97	58
500	165	125	76

Are these dimensions consistent with the tubs being geometrically similar,

(a) if the measurements are exact,

(b) if they could be wrong by up to 1mm?

(Calculate ratios $\dfrac{L}{l}$, $\dfrac{W}{w}$ and $\dfrac{H}{h}$, and consider whether they can be equal.)

Scaling up and down (continued)

12 In no.11 what should the ratio $\frac{L}{l}$ be if the tubs are similar, with masses as given?

13 A 100g jar of instant coffee is 155mm high and the lid has diameter 65mm. Calculate the height and diameter for a similar jar containing

    (a) 200g   (b) 50g.

    The actual dimensions were 188 and 80 mm for the 200g, and 126 and 54 mm for the 50g jar. Comment on any discrepancies between these and your answers to (a) and (b).

14 A 12oz jar of beetroot has height 93mm, diameter 72mm. A bigger jar is 132mm high.

    (a) If the jars are similar, find the diameter of the bigger jar, and how much it contains.

    In fact the second jar has diameter 84mm. Calculate

    (b) how much it contains, if all dimensions given are exact,

    (c) the maximum amount it could contain, if all dimensions are correct to the nearest mm, the 12oz still being exact. (The bigger jar actually had 25oz on its label.)

15 A 19oz tin of peas has height 107mm, diameter 84mm. A smaller tin has 65mm diameter.

    (a) Calculate its height and the weight of contents assuming the tins are similar.

    The second tin is in fact 93mm tall. Calculate

    (b) its weight of contents if dimensions are exact,

    (c) the maximum it could contain if all measurements could be up to 1mm wrong, assuming both tins are completely full.

16 A 1 litre carton of juice has dimensions 168, 95 and 63 mm. What should be the dimensions of a similar carton to contain 200ml?

17 A 6oz tin of evaporated milk has height 56mm, diameter 63mm. Calculate the dimensions for a similar tin to hold $14\frac{1}{2}$oz.

18 The A series of paper sizes begins with A0, which has area 1m². This can be folded in half to make A1, which is geometrically similar to A0, the width of A0 becoming the length of A1 while half the length of A0 becomes the width of A1.

    (a) Find the ratio of length to width for an A0 sheet, (and hence for A1 as well.)

    Folding again produces successively A2, A3, A4,... all of the same shape as A0.

    (b) *Calculate* the dimensions of this A4 sheet to 4SF; check by measuring.

    (c) By rounding length and width to the nearest mm obtain a rational approximation *m/n* for $\sqrt{2}$.

19 If the radius of a circle is increased by 10%, what is the ratio of the new radius to the old? What is then the ratio of new to old areas? Hence show that the area increases by 21%.

20 Find the percentage change in the circumference, surface area and volume of an object when the length is increased by

    (a) 20%

    (b) 2%

    (c) 0.2%, assuming no change of shape.

    (d) Continue with other percentage changes; see if you can find exact and approximate formulae for the percentage changes in area and volume when the length changes by *x*%.

Tangents and touching circles

1 In the figure the circle touches the sides of $\triangle ABC$ at X, Y, Z.

AB = 13cm, BC = 14cm, CA =15cm, and $\triangle ABC$ has area 84cm^2.

(a) If $BX = x$ cm, which other length $= x$? Find AY and CY in terms of x, and hence find x by forming an equation.

(b) Given that $\angle B = 67.4°$, calculate $\angle ZYX$.

(c) Find the radius r of the circle by expressing the areas of triangles IBC, ICA, IAB in terms of r and using the total area 84cm^2.

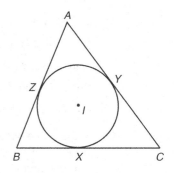

2 Use the method of no.1(c) to find the radius of the inscribed circle (touching the three sides)

(a) of a triangle with sides 3, 4, 5 cm

(b) of $\triangle ABC$ in which BC = 6.3cm, AB = 3.9cm and the altitude AD =3.6cm. Check by accurate drawing.

3 Draw $\triangle ABC$ with AB = 3cm, BC = 4.5cm, $\angle B = 90°$. Construct the circle that touches AB at A and passes through C, and measure and also calculate its radius. (NB: "touches AB" means that AB is a tangent. For the calculation, complete the rectangle $ABCD$, express the sides of $\triangle ODC$, where O is the circle's centre, in terms of the radius r, and apply Pythagoras' theorem to give an equation).

4 In the figure $\triangle ABC$ has dimensions in cm as shown, and AD is an altitude. Find BC, and prove that AB touches the circle with centre C and radius AC.

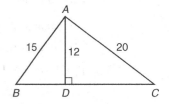

5 Three circles of radius 3cm touch each other externally. Calculate in surd form, and then to 3DP, the radii of the circles that touch them all

(a) internally,

(b) externally,

and check by drawing. (The figure takes up two thirds of a page: the centres of the given circles form an equilateral triangle.)

6 (a) Six equal circles touch a circle of radius 6cm internally, and each touches two of the others externally, like ball bearings in a race. Calculate the radius of each and check by drawing.

(b) Repeat with four touching circles instead of six, giving the answer in surd form and then to 3DP.

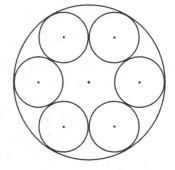

7 Use a whole page. Take the bottom printed line as x axis, with O halfway along. Draw the y axis up the page. Let S be (0, 3cm). For values of r from 1.8 to 9cm in steps of 1.2cm, draw two circles of radius r that touch the x axis and pass through S. Also draw one for r = 1.5cm. Find formulae for the coordinates of the centres in terms of r, and check them for r = 6. Draw the locus of centres. What curve is it? Try to find its equation. (This question is made assuming that you are using an exercise book with lines ruled at 0.6cm intervals. If instead the spacing is 0.5cm, then let the values of r be from 2 to 9 in steps of 1cm.)

Tangents and touching circles *(continued)*

8 *TA*, *TB* are tangents to circle c_1 of radius $r_1 = 4.5$cm, and $\angle ATB = 60°$.

(a) Calculate the radius r_2 of c_2 which touches *TA*, *TB* and c_1.

Hence find the radii of

(b) c_3, which touches *TA*, *TB* and c_2,

(c) c_0, which touches *TA* produced, *TB* produced and c_1. Check by drawing.

9 In the figure two circular arcs with centres at *B*, *C* and radius equal to *BC* = 2*a* meet at *A*. Calculate the radius of the circle that touches the arcs and *BC*, and check by measurement in the figure.

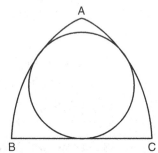

10 Draw a semicircle of radius 6cm with diameter *AB* and centre *O*. For various values of *r*, from 0.5 or 0.6 up to 3 (depending on the spacing of the lines in your book), draw two circles of radius *r* that touch *AB* and touch the semicircle. Sketch the locus of centres and try to find its equation, taking *O* as origin.

11 Draw a circle *C*, with centre *O* and radius 6cm, and mark a point *S* 4cm to the right of *O*. For *r* = 1, 1.2, 2, 3, 4, 4.8, 5 cm draw one or, if possible, two circles of radius *r* to pass through *S* and touch *C*. Mark the centres of these circles clearly and sketch the curve on which they lie.

12 Two circles with centres *A*, *B* touch each other at *T*.

PQ, *UV* and *TM* are common tangents.

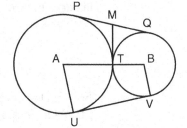

(a) Prove that *PM* = *MQ*, that $\angle PTQ = 90°$ and that $\angle AMB = 90°$.

(b) If *AT* = *a* cm, *BT* = *b* cm find *UV* by using $\triangle BAX$ with *BX* $\perp$ *AU*.

(c) Show that if *a* and *b* are squares of whole numbers then *UV* is a whole number of cm. Is the converse true?

(d) Use the answer to (b) to find the radius of the circle that touches *UV* and the given circles.

13 Five coins of radius *a* lie in a square frame with one at each corner and one in the centre. Find the minimum possible side of the frame.

14 Nine spheres of radius *a* are packed in a cubical box, one in each corner and one in the centre. What percentage of the volume do they occupy?

15 In the figure two circles with centres *A*, *B* touch each other externally at *C* and touch the big circle internally.

Calculate the area inside the big circle that is outside the smaller circles, given that the common tangent *ST* has length 2*l*. Check your answer by considering the special case in which the two smaller circles are equal.

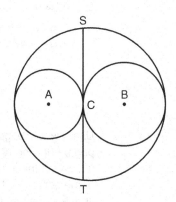

16 Explain how you would construct

(a) a circle to touch internally three equal given circles,

(b) (harder!) a triangle *ABC* given the length of *BC*, the size of angle *A*, and the inradius (the radius of the incircle, which touches the three sides of the triangle.)

Shapes and surds

1 For an equilateral triangle of side *a* calculate the altitude, the area, and the distance of the centre from each vertex, and from each side, all in surd form.

2 In the hexagon of side *a* calculate in surd form

(a) the area ABCDEF

(b) AC

(c) PQ

(d) the area of PQRSTU as a fraction of ABCDEF.

Use your answers to write down without further detailed working

(e) PR

(f) the side of the hexagon formed when PR, QS, RT, SU, TP are joined,

(g) the area of this hexagon as a fraction of ABCDEF.

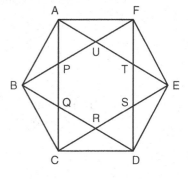

3 The diagram on the right shows the 'tangram' dissection of a square of side 4*a*. All angles are 90° or 45°, and P, Q, X, U, K, V are mid-points of AB, BC, PQ, AK, AC, KC. Find, in surd form where necessary,

(a) PQ, XK, UX,

(b) the areas QVC, PBQ, XQVK, PXUA.

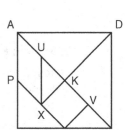

4 The octagon on the right is regular with AB = *a*.

(a) Find AD and hence show that
$$\tan 22\tfrac{1}{2}° = \frac{1}{\sqrt{2}+1} = \sqrt{2}-1.$$

(b) Find AE using Pythagoras' theorem in △ADE, and show that
$$\sin 22\tfrac{1}{2}° = (4+2\sqrt{2})^{-\frac{1}{2}}.$$
Check this using a calculator.

(c) Calculate the area of the octagon

(i) by finding areas of ABP, BPQC, PQRS,

(ii) by using your answer to (b) and the formula "$\tfrac{1}{2}bc\sin A$" to find △OAH.
The answers should agree!

5 (a) Find the area of a hexagon ABCDEF in which each side is *a* and angles A, C, E are right angles.

(b) A square ABCD of side *a* has equilateral triangles ABP, BCQ, CDR, DAS drawn outside it. Find the areas of △PBQ and of PQRS.

Shapes and surds *(continued)*

6   (a) If the pattern of equal regular octagons on the left is extended in all directions, what fraction of the plane is covered? How big could this fraction be made by rearranging the octagons?

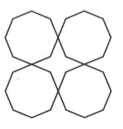

    (b) Each dot in the pattern on the right is distant *a* from its six nearest neighbours. Find the average density of dots per unit area.

7   **Extending a hexagon to a dodecagon**

    Warning: this figure takes up nearly 12cm height and 12cm width on the page. Draw a regular hexagon of side *a* about 3cm, draw 6 squares of side *a*, each stuck to one side of the hexagon, then draw a rubber band fitting tightly round the figure.

    (a) Find, with reasons, the angle between two neighbouring straight pieces of rubber band and explain why all the pieces are equal in length. (They are thus the sides of a regular dodecagon.)

    (b) Calculate the perimeter and area of the dodecagon in terms of *a*, using surds where necessary.

    (c) Draw the smallest possible circle round the dodecagon; let its radius be *R* and centre O. Find the area of the dodecagon in terms of *R* by considering the triangle formed by O and two neighbouring vertices of the dodecagon. Use your answer to show that π is greater than 3.

    (d) By comparing the area formulae you have found in (b) and (c) show that $R = \sqrt{2 + \sqrt{3}}\,a$. Check by measurement on your figure.

Notes and Answers

G1 Areas, angles and constructions

The use of graph paper gives a precision to the location of the figures, as well as enabling the "crate minus packing" technique shown in no. 12.

All units are cm² in 1 to 12.

| 1 | 18 | 3 | 10.5 | 5 | 1.5 | 7 | 6 | 9 | 7.5 | 11 | 32 |
| 2 | 9 | 4 | 3 | 6 | 4.5 | 8 | 10.5 | 10 | 8 | | |

12 13.5; the crate is 30, the packing triangles are 3, 6 and 7.5.

Angles are given in alphabetical order to 1DP, though such precision is not expected in measurements

13 22cm², 74.7°, 57.5°, 47.7°, 180°

14 17cm², 41.8°, 67.6°, 70.6°, 180°

15 42cm², 49.4°, 130.6°, 360°; it's a parallelogram.

16 20cm², 43.6°, 136.4°, 360°; a rhombus.

17 (a) (4, 18.6)   (b) 64.5°   (c) 5.02, 6.10 cm

18 F is (15.2, 11.8). ∠F = 37°. DF = 8.10cm, EF = 5.34cm

19 (a) K (3.6, 10.0), N (7, 12)   (b) 142.5°, 99.5°   (c) 3.95cm

20 (a) It's *at* A

(b) 090°, 234°, 018°, 162°, 306° (keep adding 144; subtract 360 when necessary)

(c) 37.08km (perimeter of a regular pentagon.)

G2 Draw and investigate

This sheet begins the exploration of geometrical shapes and ideas, continued in later sheets. A setsquare with built-in protractor is useful, but not essential, for the drawing.

1 (a) $\triangle OBP$ is $\frac{1}{2}$ of square $OABP$, and is $\frac{1}{4}$ of square $OBCQ$, so the area of $OBCQ$ is 2 times the area of $OABP$. Likewise $OCDR$'s area is 2 times that of $OBCQ$.

(b) Areas are 1, 2, 4, 8, 16, 32 cm². Sides are 1, 1.41, 2. 2.83, 4, 5.66 cm

2 (a) The lines bisect the angles. Where they meet is 3km from the coast.

(b) AC = 15km. Ratios of sides for $\triangle ABC$ are 9:12:15 = 3:4:5. For the inside triangles the sides are 6, 8, 10 km and 3, 4, 5 km, still in the ratio 3:4:5.

(c) $36 + 2\pi = 42.3$km, $36 + 4\pi = 48.6$km. (Each journey has three straight parts parallel and equal to the three sides, joined up by circular arcs centred on the corners. Since Scott altogether turns through 360° in going round the three corners, the circular arcs would make a complete circle.)

3 (a) 6km

(b) 36 small triangles; perimeter of each is $\frac{1}{6}$ of the island's perimeter, area of each is $\frac{1}{36}$ of the island's area.

(c) 36km, except for Manoj's, which is 18km.

(d) Manoj's, Linda's.

G3 Exploring triangles

I had been teaching for some years before I discovered that the altitude of an equilateral triangle is almost exactly $\frac{13}{15}$ of a side. This, along with other properties of triangle, including the angle sum, is explored in this sheet.

1 (a) 5.2cm, $\frac{13}{15} = 0.87$ (c) 60°, 60°, 60°, 30°, 120°

(b) $\frac{1}{2}, \frac{2}{3}$

2 (a) 6.5cm, then as in no.1.

3 (a) 3, 3.9,3.9 cm, half the length of the sides.   (d) 45.2°, 67.4°, 67.4°, 180°

(b) $\frac{2}{3}, \frac{1}{2}$ (e) both 22.6°

(c) 7.2, 5.54, 5.54 cm; meet 5.95cm from A (f) both 43.2cm², both 2 × area.

4   (a) 3.5, 3.25, 3.75 cm, half the side lengths.

    (b) $\frac{2}{3}$, $\frac{1}{2}$

    (c) 6, 6.46, 5.6 cm, 4.125cm from A

    (d) 59.5°, 53.1°, 67.4°, 180°

    (e) both 36.9°, because Δs BAD, BCF share $\angle B$, have

        a right angle each and have same angle sum.

    (f) Both products are 42cm², same reason as before.

5   (a) equilateral, isosceles, scalene

    (b) when Δ is equilateral

    (c) when it's isosceles

    (d) always 180° (One way: put a pencil along BC, pointing from B to C. Turn it about C through $\angle C$, so it is along AC, pointing from A to C. Then turn it about A through $\angle A$, then through $\angle B$ about B. It ends up along BC but pointing from C to B, so it has turned 180° in total.)

    (e) It's a half scale version of the original triangle.

6   Sides should be 6.77cm each; the triangle is equilateral (but may not seem exactly so!)

7   (a) at Q_1

    (b) 0.5km apart

    (c) It is halved; just as distance along a 60° slope is double the horizontal distance, because the slope distance and the horizontal distance make one half of an equilateral triangle.

    (d) 0.0625km or 62.5m apart

    (e) practically at Q_1, Q_2 and Q_3.

G4 Starting vectors and Pythagoras

This sheet introduces the important ideas of vectors in a natural way, then goes on, using the "crate minus packing" technique already seen in G1 "Areas, angles and constructions on graph paper" to develop a way of calculating the length of a vector with given coordinates, i.e. to derive Pythagoras' theorem. Some exercises on this come at the end. I used this sheet with an able class of 12–13 year olds and had a visiting inspector full of enthusiasm about the fact that a class as young as this could discover for themselves the most important theorem in mathematics! The work on vectors can also help with some of the questions in the next sheet, "Parallelograms."

1   A square, centre (2, 10)

2   Parallelogram, centre (–7, 11.5)

3   Isosceles right-angled triangle, no centre (in the sense of a centre of rotational symmetry)

4   Kite, no centre

5   Octagon, centre (–6, 4) [Is it regular? No.]

6 $\begin{pmatrix}-2\\1\end{pmatrix}$, $\begin{pmatrix}-2\\-1\end{pmatrix}$, rhombus, (1, –3)

7 $\begin{pmatrix}-2\\-2\end{pmatrix}$, $\begin{pmatrix}-3\\3\end{pmatrix}$, rectangle, (–6.5, –5.5)

8 $\begin{pmatrix}-1\\3\end{pmatrix}$, $\begin{pmatrix}-4\\-4\end{pmatrix}$, parallelogram, (3.5, –7.5)

9 $\begin{pmatrix}-4\\-2\end{pmatrix}$, $\begin{pmatrix}1\\2\end{pmatrix}$, parallelogram, (–6.5, –10)

10 $\begin{pmatrix}1\\2\end{pmatrix}\begin{pmatrix}-2\\1\end{pmatrix}\begin{pmatrix}-1\\-2\end{pmatrix}$, (7.5, 4.5) or $\begin{pmatrix}-1\\-2\end{pmatrix}\begin{pmatrix}-2\\1\end{pmatrix}\begin{pmatrix}1\\2\end{pmatrix}$, (6.5, 2.5)

11 $\begin{pmatrix}-1\\3\end{pmatrix}\begin{pmatrix}3\\1\end{pmatrix}\begin{pmatrix}1\\-3\end{pmatrix}$, (7, –2) or $\begin{pmatrix}1\\-3\end{pmatrix}\begin{pmatrix}3\\1\end{pmatrix}\begin{pmatrix}-1\\3\end{pmatrix}$, (8, –5)

12 (a) $\begin{pmatrix}-30\\-50\end{pmatrix}$

     (b) $\begin{pmatrix}-50\\30\end{pmatrix}\begin{pmatrix}50\\-30\end{pmatrix}\begin{pmatrix}-20\\80\end{pmatrix}$ or $\begin{pmatrix}50\\-30\end{pmatrix}\begin{pmatrix}-50\\30\end{pmatrix}\begin{pmatrix}80\\20\end{pmatrix}$

13 (a) $\begin{pmatrix}-a\\-b\end{pmatrix}$

     (b) $\begin{pmatrix}-b\\a\end{pmatrix}\begin{pmatrix}b\\-a\end{pmatrix}\begin{pmatrix}a-b\\a+b\end{pmatrix}$ or $\begin{pmatrix}b\\-a\end{pmatrix}\begin{pmatrix}-b\\a\end{pmatrix}\begin{pmatrix}a+b\\b-a\end{pmatrix}$

14 $\begin{pmatrix} 7 \\ 10 \end{pmatrix}\begin{pmatrix} 2 \\ 2 \end{pmatrix}; \begin{pmatrix} 7 \\ 1 \end{pmatrix}\begin{pmatrix} -7 \\ -1 \end{pmatrix}\begin{pmatrix} 2 \\ -7 \end{pmatrix}\begin{pmatrix} -2 \\ 7 \end{pmatrix}\begin{pmatrix} -5 \\ -8 \end{pmatrix}\begin{pmatrix} 5 \\ 8 \end{pmatrix}$

15 (a) $\begin{pmatrix} -9 \\ 10 \end{pmatrix}\begin{pmatrix} -3 \\ 5 \end{pmatrix}\begin{pmatrix} 6 \\ -5 \end{pmatrix}\begin{pmatrix} -6 \\ 5 \end{pmatrix}$ (b) $\begin{pmatrix} -9 \\ -5 \end{pmatrix}\begin{pmatrix} -1 \\ -3 \end{pmatrix}\begin{pmatrix} -8 \\ -2 \end{pmatrix}\begin{pmatrix} 8 \\ 2 \end{pmatrix}$

16 q – p, p – q

17 10, 3.16

18 (10) 5, 2.24   (11) 10, 3.16

19 169, 13

20 (a) 25, 5

    (b) 13, 3.61

    (c) 8, 2.83

21 Crate $(a + b)^2$, packing $2ab$, sloping square $a^2 + b^2$. Square of hypotenuse = sum of squares of other two sides.

22 (a) 17   (c) 2.24   (e) 6, 5.20
    (b) 20   (d) 5.66

23 $x = \pm 7$, $y = \pm 20$

24 18m

25 141mm, 104mm

26 (9, 10) (9, –6)

27 $OP = QR = \sqrt{45} = 6.71$,
    $OR = PQ = \sqrt{5} = 2.24$,
    $OQ = PR = \sqrt{50} = 7.07$. It's a rectangle.

G5 Parallelograms

No.1 is basic exploratory work, discovering different sorts of parallelograms and their properties. Nos. 2 and 3 use what has been discovered to help locate missing parts of parallelograms. Ideas on vectors are helpful here, but not indispensable. No.4 is a challenging reasoning test. The rest of the sheet gives more routine practice, though some of the later ones are quite challenging. Some of these are from the classic textbook *A New Geometry for Schools* by the renowned C V Durell.

1 Answers are either exact, or given to 2DP for lengths and 1DP for angles, but such accuracy is not expected from drawing.

(a)
Part	AB	∠B	Type	AK	AC	BK	BD	∠AKD	∠DBC
1st	2.5	30°	general	2.02	4.03	4.13	8.26	153.2°	8.7°
2nd	6	30°	rhombus	1.55	3.11	5.80	11.59	90°	15°
3rd	2.5	60°	general	2.61	5.22	3.78	7.57	138.9°	16.6°
4th	6	60°	rhombus	3	6	5.20	10.39	90°	30°
5th	2.5	90°	rectangle	3.25	6.5	3.25	6.5	134.8°	22.6°
6th	6	90°	square	4.24	8.49	4.24	8.49	90°	45°

(b) See the Type column above.

(c) The diagonals bisect each other in every parallelogram.
They are equal in length when the parallelogram is a rectangle (that includes squares.)
They are perpendicular when the parallelogram is a rhombus (including squares.)
They bisect the angles when the parallelogram is a rhombus (including squares.)

2 All the coordinates work out as whole numbers when calculated, but results from drawing will not necessarily reflect this. The same applies to no.3.

(a) $A(94, 196)$ $D(128, 196)$
(b) $A(26, 200)$ $D(62, 200)$
(c) $C(68, 130)$ $D(68, 144)$
(d) $C(124, 110)$ $D(134, 134)$
(e) $B(16, 90)$ $C(40, 80)$ $D(64, 90)$
(f) $B(98, 84)$ $D(134, 84)$
(g) $A(40, 58)$ $B(20, 10)$ $D(64, 48)$
(h) $A(112, 42)$ $C(128, 18)$ $D(150, 50)$

3 (a) (112, 90), (48, 170), (104, 150) They are the midpoints of the sides; likewise in (b).
(b) (20, 160), (60, 120), (80, 140)
(c) $A(34, 124)$ $B(6, 56)$ $C(54, 76)$
(d) $A(110, 50)$ $B(130, 110)$ $C(90, 110)$
(e) $A(50, 65)$ $B(50, 5)$ $C(130, 5)$

4   The search for counter-examples is the important part of this question. In the cases where the statement is true, (so no counter-example exists) the pupil's ability to give a proof, and the nature of the proof, will depend on whether and how proof in geometry has been taught.

(a) False. Draw two equal lines crossing but not bisecting each other; make them the diagonals.

(b) True

(c) False; draw perpendicular lines crossing but not bisecting each other, to be diagonals.

(d) True

(e) True

(f) False: it could be an isosceles trapezium.

(g) True

(h) True

(i) False: Draw triangles ABD and BCD with $AB = CD$, BD common and $\angle A = \angle C$, but such that the triangles are *not* congruent; this is possible because the equal angles are not included.

(j) (1) True (2) False: a kite provides a counter-example.

(k) True

(l) True

5   (a) 54°   (b) 27°   (c) 144°

6   $67\frac{1}{2}°$, $22\frac{1}{2}°$

7   150°

8   (a) 36°, 72°   (b) and (c) proofs

9   proofs

10 proof

11 Start with the diagonal BP drawn at 45° to BC, meeting AC at P. 4cm.

(A challenging extension: Given $\triangle ABC$ with acute angles at B, C, construct a square with two corners on BC and one each on AB and AC. This can be related to the question just dealt with.)

G6 Regular Polygons

Regular hexagons, octagons, pentagons and dodecagons: their symmetric beauties and some of their hidden relationships are the subject of this sheet. No advanced knowledge is presupposed, but some of the questions will stretch able young minds.

1   (a) 60°   (b) 60°   (c) 6cm

2   (a) 120°   (b) 30°   (c) 30°   (d) 120°

3   (a) 10.4cm   (b) Because $PQ = BP = AP = QC$: 26/45

4   (a) They are equal because both are equilateral and have PU as a common side

(b) They are equal because $BP = PU$ and the heights are the same

(c) $\frac{1}{3}$

(d) They are not exactly equal: $\frac{1}{3}$ is correct because not based on measurement

5   $ACDE + ABC + AFE$

6   PA 2.4cm, area 55.72cm²

7   (a) 135°   (b) 22.5°   (c) 45°   (d) 90°

8   (a) 22.5°   (b) 90°   (c) 45°

9   2

10 (a) 108°; 36°   (b) 36°; 36°

11 Pentagon

	Side/mm	Diagonal/mm	Flame length/mm	Side + flame length/mm
P1	55	89	89	144
P2	21	34	34	55
P3	8	13	13	21
P4	3	5	5	8

   (a) Diagonal = flame length: $AI = IG$ because $\triangle AIG$ has equal angles at A and G; 89mm.

   (b) See last column in table; side + flame length = side of previous polygon; e.g. $HI + IB = AB$ because $\triangle ABH$ has equal angles at A and H.

12 (a) P1: 1.6182, P2: 1.6190, P3: 1.625. They should be exactly equal, because the shapes are geometrically similar, but measurements are not exact.

   (b) $\triangle$s ABH, AIH are similar, so have same shape ratios. $AB = tAH = t \times tIH = t^2IH$.

   (c) $BH = BI + IH = AI + IH = tIH + IH = (t + 1)IH$. But $AH = BH$, so $t^2 = t + 1$.

   (d) 1.6180

   (e) P1: 0.6180, P2: 0.6176, P3: 0.6154. They seem to be $t - 1$; this is because these ratios should be $\frac{1}{t}$, and the equation $t^2 = t + 1$, when divided by t gives $t = 1 + \frac{1}{t}$.

13 (a) 15°, 15° and 150°; 6cm; there are 24

                                              (c) $\frac{3}{4}$ of the square = 108cm²

   (b) 4 equilateral and 8 isosceles triangles, like those inside the dodecagon.

                                              (d) $3r^2$, less than the circle which is πr^2.

G7 Enemy Territory

This sheet was a favourite "near end of term" exercise for 13 year olds, but can be used at any time, and with older pupils. It revises bearings and brings in ideas about locus, but in a context that makes the children think hard about how the given information can be translated into drawing.

1 8.94km, 026.6°

2 5.10km, 191.3°

3 (4, 10)

4 (9, 2)

5 (7, 11) or (12.55, 8.3)

6 (9.8, 15.3) or (5.1, 17.95)

7 (2.0, 19.75)

8 (5, 14)

9 (9, 8.4) or (9, 3.6)

10 (2, 11)

11 (6.8, 8.6)

12 (9, 10.5)

13 (3, 5)

14 (10.0, 16.55)

15 J is at (9.8, 15.3), I at (7, 11), P at (9, 8.4)

G8 Reflections

Reflection is the most basic Euclidean (i.e. size and shape conserving) transformation, as all the others can be obtained by combining reflections. Reflection is also associated with symmetry, which has both aesthetic and mathematical importance. This sheet gives practice in doing reflections and seeing axes of symmetry; it also investigates the result of combining two reflections.

1 (a) (5, 16)

   (b) (29, 16)

   (c) F_2 and F_3 face left, F_1 faces right. Translation 24**i**.

   (d) (25, 6) and (29, 6)

   (e) F_4 is more like F_2, F_5 more like F_1.

   (f) Half turn about D. Not a reflection.

   (g) (8, 33)

2 B (6, 40) C (5, 28) D (18, 27) E (20, 12) F (27, 7) G (35, 29)

3 (a) It reflects into itself   (b) Yes, in SQ.   (c) A (13, 4) C (17, 26)

4 (a) (14, 8) and (14, 17)

   (b) Reflection in $x = 7\frac{1}{2}$ or in $y = 12\frac{1}{2}$; or rotation about $(7\frac{1}{2}, 12\frac{1}{2})$ through $-73.7°$ or $+106.3°$.

5 (a) 1   (c) 4   (e) 2   (g) 6

    (b) 3   (d) 0   (f) 2

6 (a) (51, 48) (61, 28) Translation $16\mathbf{i} - 32\mathbf{j}$.

    (b) (36, 53) (56, 13) Translation $16\mathbf{i} - 32\mathbf{j}$

    (c) Translation $8\mathbf{i} - 16\mathbf{j}$, which is half the final answer in (a) and (b).

    (d) F_3; translation $24\mathbf{i}$, double the shortest movement from AB to CD.

The effect of two successive reflections in parallel mirrors is double the shortest translation that takes the first mirror to the second.

    (e) (15, 30); half turn about (30, 45)

    (f) (20, 45); the effect of two successive reflections in two perpendicular mirrors is a half turn about the point of intersection of the mirrors. 1(f) confirms it.

    (g) They are at M_3M_1T and M_3M_1F. $M_1M_3 = M_3M_1$.

    (h) M_1M_2 is $-16\mathbf{i} + 32\mathbf{j}$, the inverse of M_2M_1

G9 Calculating π

Before I started teaching, having done a maths degree and a Ph D, I had no idea how π could be calculated in a way that would be accessible to school pupils. I first devised a rather more complicated approach, which was later modified, with help from Adrian Freed, a bright young student at the school where I taught. The sheet has answers included at the bottom.

G10 Similar shapes

The advent of modern reprographic and computer imaging techniques has made the notions of enlarging or stretching a figure much more familiar than formerly. Accordingly this sheet begins with computer images that have been transformed in such ways; the student is required by measuring to find out what has been done. This leads on to the idea of similarity of two figures, especially of triangles, then to some fairly familiar applications, plus some that are quite challenging.

1 In this question we are not concerned with changes of position, so there is no mention of translations, nor is any centre of enlargement specified.

    (a) Enlargement × 1.5   (d) Enlargement × 1.5, rotation +24°

    (b) Stretches: $x \times 1.5$, $y \times 1.25$ (e) Stretch: $x \times 1.2$, rotation −35°

    (c) Stretches: $x \times 1.2$, $y \times 1.5$

    (a) and (d) are similar to the original, (b) and (e) are similar to each other.

2 Similar to original: (a), (e), (f). Too fat: (c). Too thin: (b), (d).

    (a) Enlargement × 0.8, rotation +18°   (e) Enlargement × 0.6, rotation −85°

    (b) Stretches: $x \times -1$ (a reflection), $y \times 0.9$ (f) Enlargement × 0.85, rotation 180°

    (c) Stretches: $x \times 0.8$, $y \times 1.3$; rotation −21°

    (d) Stretches: $x \times -0.8$, $y \times 0.72$ (hard to get accurately by measurement, as heights are not big in the figures.)

    (b) and (d) are similar to each other, not to the original.

3 (a) Enlargement × 1.5   (d) Enlargement × 0.8, rotation +20°

    (b) Stretch: $y \times 1.5$ (e) In (a) and (d), enlargements

    (c) Stretch: $x \times 1.2$ (f) Same as (e)

4 (a) No, basically because the shape of a triangle is determined by its angles. Euclid proved this via intercept theorems. A more practical, if less rigorous, way might be as follows: Suppose *ABC* is similar to *PQR* (with *P* corresponding to *A*, *Q* to *B* and *R* to *C*). Make a copy on acetate of *PQR*, enlarged just enough to make the new *PQ* the same length as *AB*. Now put this new *PQR* on top of *ABC*, with *P* on *A* and *PQ* along *AB*. *Q* then lands on *B*, and since the triangles are equiangular (and enlargement doesn't change angles) *QR* will lie along *BC*, while also *PR* lies along *AC*. Thus *R* lies on *C*, and the enlarged version of *PQR* is congruent to *ABC*. But enlargement increases all lengths in the same proportion, whence the result.

(b) A square and an oblong rectangle satisfy (1) and not (2). A square and a non-square rhombus satisfy (2) but not (1).

5   40ft

6   14m

7   (a) $5\frac{1}{3}$cm, $22\frac{1}{2}$cm   (b) 45m

8   $96\frac{7}{8}$

9   (a) *ABC, DBA, DAC*   (b) 12cm   (c) 7, 24, 6.72m
    (d) Follows from similarity of inner triangles to whole triangle. Use $x + y = a$ and multiply by a to get Pythagoras' theorem.

10 (a) 4cm   (b) 1/40, 2/5

11 (a) 20cm   (b) 240, 260 cm   (c) Proof

12 1.6180

G11 Locus: Where are the points?

This subject offers great scope for mathematical reasoning and investigation. In this sheet the main locus results are discovered by the pupil, and then applied to find points from given clues. Questions with a star * are more challenging than the rest.

1   (a) A quarter of a circle   (c) a circle with centre at the centre of the fixed penny
    (b) a straight line segment parallel to the chute   (d) a cycloid

2   (a) On a circle, centre *A*, radius 5cm.
    (b) 8cm
    (c) It is straight, makes 90° with *AB*, meets *AB* at its midpoint.
    (d) The perpendicular bisector of the line segment joining the two points.

3   (a) They are on two lines parallel to *l* and 1cm away from *l*. This pair of lines is the locus.
    (b) 4
    (c) 30° and 120°
    (d) the pair of bisectors of the angles between the lines
    (e) A line parallel to the two given lines, and half way between them.

4   The locus consists of three quarter circles, with radii 3, $3\sqrt{2}$ and 3 cm; length 16.1cm

5   (a) A circle on *AB* as diameter. The diagonals are equal and bisect each other at *M*, the midpoint of *AB*. Hence *PM* is always half the length of *AB*, so locus of *P* is a circle with centre *M*.
    (b) A pair of straight lines parallel to *AB* and 2.4cm away from *AB*.
    (c) 4, 2.53cm, 7.59cm

6   (a) $x = 3$ 8   (a) $y = \pm 3$
    (b) $y = 2$ (b) $x = 5, x = 7$
    (c) (3, 2)   (c) (5, 3) (5, −3) (7, 3) (7, −3)
    (d) $y = \frac{1}{2}x + 3\frac{1}{2}$
    (e) (−3, 2)

7   (a) $y = \pm x$ 9   (a) Drawing
    (b) $y = 6 - x$ (b) (−3, −3) (−6, −6)
                            (c) $(-3 \pm \sqrt{5}, -4) = (-0.764, -4), (-5.236, -4)$

10 (a) Drawing
    (b) a quarter circle, centre *O*; diagonals of rectangle are equal and bisect, so *OM* = 5m for all positions of the ladder.
    (c) (6, 1.5) $x_Q = x_M \times \frac{3}{2}$, $y_Q = y_M \times \frac{1}{2}$; horizontal and vertical stretches with factors $\frac{3}{2}$ and $\frac{1}{2}$ respectively, (making the locus part of an ellipse.)

11 Parabola

Notes and Answers

G12 Exotic locations – Loci with Cabri II

This sheet is very Cabri-dependent as written, and needs some of the special files that come with the program, including some I made for nos. 4 to 6. These can be downloaded free from www.tarquinbooks.com – simply key VMW into the search box and follow the links on the product page. The files work on Cabri II or Cabri III. It is, however, a fascinating and very "hands-on" way of discovering interesting loci. Answers are not needed.

G13 Scaling up and down

This important topic is highly counter-intuitive for most pupils; they are convinced that all variables are related by direct proportion. The sheet begins with some discovery work in which they find that it's not as simple as that; by no.4 they are hopefully able to formulate the fact that area ratios are the square, and volume ratios the cube, of the ratios of corresponding lengths in geometrically similar objects.

For some of the later questions I visited a supermarket with a ruler. In these questions the calculated answers don't exactly match the reality on the shelf; but that's typical of the relationship between mathematics and the real world!

1 $1:25:400:x^2$, $1:125:8000:x^3$

2 Heights 10, 15, $5x$ cm; areas 10π, 40π, 90π, $x^2\pi$ cm^2; volumes 5π, 40π, 135π, $5x^3\pi$ cm^3.
Ratios $1:2:3:x$, $1:4:9:x^2$, $1:8:27:x^3$.

3 16, 32, 48 cm; 12, 48, 108 cm^2; 1:2:3, 1:4:9

4 (a) $m^2:n^2$ (b) $m^3:n^3$

5 (a) 10^6 (b) 10^9 (c) 10^{-4} (d) 10^{-6} (e) 10^1

6 (a) $12m^2$ (b) $4.5cm^3$

7 (a) $2\sqrt{2}$cm, $\frac{1}{2}$cm^2 (b) $2\sqrt{2}d$ cm, $\frac{d^2}{2}$ cm^2

8 $2h\sqrt{3}$cm, $\frac{\sqrt{3}}{3}h^2$ cm^2

9 $4.828a^2$

10 (a) 6.12cm, 173cm^2, 118cm^3 (b) $0.612x$ cm, $1.73x^2$cm^2, $0.118x^3$cm^3

11 (a) No   (b) Yes; L/l 1.2519 to 1.2868, W/w 1.2653 to 1.3125, H/h 1.2712 to 1.3509; the greatest of the minimum ratios, 1.2712, is below the lowest of the maximum ratios, 1.2868.

12 1.26

13 (a) 195, 81.9 mm (both more than actual dimensions)
(b) 123, 51.6 mm (both less than actual dimensions). Perhaps the bigger jars are filled proportionally more, so that they can be smaller than expected.

14 (a) 102mm, 34.3oz   (b) 23.2oz   (c) 24.0oz

15 (a) 82.8mm, 8.80oz   (b) 9.89oz   (c) 10.7oz

16 98.2, 55.6, 36.8 mm

17 75.1, 84.5 mm

18 (a) $\sqrt{2}$ (b) 297.3, 210.2 mm   (c) 99/70

19 11:10, 121:100

20 (a) 20%, 44%, 72.8%   (b) 2%, 4.04%. 6.1208%   (c) 0.2%, 0.4004%, 0.6012008%
(d) Area change is $(2x + \frac{x^2}{100})$%, which approximates $2x$% when x is small.

Volume change is $(3x + \frac{3x^2}{100} + \frac{x^3}{10000})$%, approximately $3x$% for small x.

Notes and Answers

G14 Tangents and touching circles

Tangents and touching circles provide a very rich field for problem setting and solving. Many of the drawing questions can well be done using geometry software. The calculations give scope for the use of algebra.

1 (a) BY; $13 - x$, $14 - x$, $x = 6$ (b) 56.3°   (c) 4cm

2 (a) 1cm   (b) 1.4cm

3 3.25cm

4 25cm; use converse of Pythagoras.

5 (a) $2\sqrt{3} + 3 = 6.464$cm   (b) $2\sqrt{3} - 3 = 0.464$cm

6 (a) 2cm   (b) $\dfrac{6}{1 + \sqrt{2}} = 2.485$ cm

7 $(\sqrt{6r - 9}, r)$ Parabola, $y = \dfrac{x^2 + 9}{6}$.

8 (a) 1.5cm   (b) 0.5cm   (c) 13.5cm

9 $\frac{3}{4}a$

10 $y = 3 - \dfrac{x^2}{12}$.

11 (The curve is an ellipse with foci at O and S.)

12 (a) Proofs   (c) Proof; converse is not true

   (b) $2\sqrt{ab}$ (d) $\dfrac{ab}{a + b + 2\sqrt{ab}}$

(Let the circle touch UV at W and have radius r; then UW and WV can be found using the result of (b); their total is $2\sqrt{ab}$, which gives an equation for r.)

13 $2(1 + \sqrt{2})a$

14 47.1%

15 $\frac{1}{2}\pi l^2$

16 (a) Let the circles have centres A, B, C and radius r. Construct the circumcentre O of $\triangle ABC$. Let the circumradius be R. Draw a circle with centre O and radius $R + r$.

   (b) Draw BC; let the inradius be r and the incentre I; it has to lie on a line parallel to BC and distance r from it. Draw this line. (There are two, but we'll take the one above BC.) Since I is where the angle bisectors meet, $\angle IBC + \angle ICB = \frac{1}{2}(\angle B + \angle C) = 90° - \frac{1}{2}\angle A$. Hence $\angle BIC = 90° + \frac{1}{2}\angle A$, which is known as $\angle A$ is given. This locates I on an arc of a circle with chord BC, the arc subtending an angle $180° + A$ at the centre. Draw this arc, choose one of the points where it meets the line r above BC; that locates I. It is then straightforward to construct BA and CA to meet at A.

G15 Shapes and surds

This sheet exercises geometrical insights and fluency in calculation with exact surds.

1 $\dfrac{a\sqrt{3}}{2}$, $\dfrac{a^2\sqrt{3}}{4}$, $\dfrac{a\sqrt{3}}{3}$, $\dfrac{a\sqrt{3}}{6}$

2 (a) $(\dfrac{3\sqrt{3}}{2})a^2$ (c) $a\sqrt{3}/3$ (e) a (g) 1/9

   (b) $a\sqrt{3}$ (d) 1/3   (f) $a/3$

3 (a) $2\sqrt{2}a$, $a\sqrt{2}$, $2a$ (b) a^2, $2a^2$, $2a^2$, $2a^2$

4 (a) $a(1 + \sqrt{2})$ (b) $a\sqrt{4 + 2\sqrt{2}}$ (c) both $2(1 + \sqrt{2})a^2$

5 (a) $\frac{1}{2}(3 + \sqrt{3})a^2$ (b) $\frac{1}{4}a^2$, $(2 + \sqrt{3})a^2$

6 (a) $\sqrt{2}/2 = 0.7071$, $2(\sqrt{2} - 1) = 0.828$, by making neighbouring octagons touch along sides.

   (b) $\dfrac{2\sqrt{3}}{3a^2}$ dots per unit area.

© tarquin publications   Venture Mathematics Worksheets   9

7 (a) 150°; triangles outside the hexagon are equilateral

(b) $12a$, $3(2 + \sqrt{3})a^2$

(c) $3R^2$; circle area is πR^2 and is greater.